YORK N

General Editors: 
of Stirling) & Prof
University of Beir

William Shakespeare

# TROILUS AND CRESSIDA

*Notes by Daniel Massa*

MA (MALTA) PH D (EDINBURGH)
*Lecturer in English, University of Malta*

**LONGMAN YORK PRESS**

YORK PRESS
Immeuble Esseily, Place Riad Solh, Beirut.

LONGMAN GROUP UK LIMITED
*Longman House, Burnt Mill, Harlow,*
*Essex CM20 2JE, England*
*Associated companies, branches and representatives*
*throughout the world*

© Librairie du Liban 1980

First published 1980
Second impression 1991

ISBN 0-582-78225-2

Produced by Longman Group (FE) Ltd.
Printed in Hong Kong

# Contents

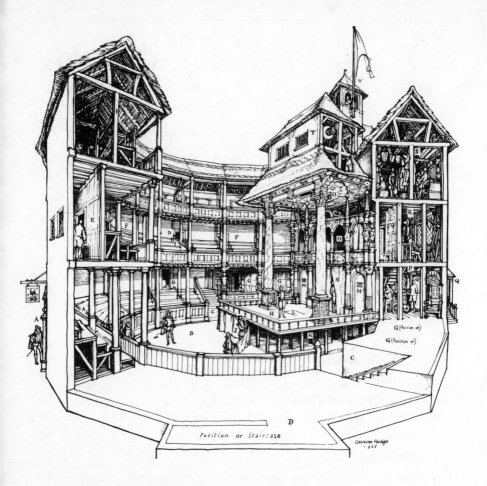

Position or Staircase

C.Walter Hodges
1965

## A CONJECTURAL RECONSTRUCTION OF THE INTERIOR OF
## THE GLOBE PLAYHOUSE

AA Main entrance
 B The Yard
CC Entrances to lowest gallery
 D Entrance to staircase and upper galleries
 E Corridor serving the different sections of the middle gallery
 F Middle gallery ('Twopenny Rooms')
 G 'Gentlemen's Rooms or Lords Rooms'
 H The stage
 J The hanging being put up round the stage
 K The 'Hell' under the stage
 L The stage trap, leading down to the Hell
MM Stage doors

N Curtained 'place behind the stage'
O Gallery above the stage, used as required sometimes by musicians, sometimes by spectators, and often as part of the play
P Back-stage area (the tiring-house)
Q Tiring-house door
R Dressing-rooms
S Wardrobe and storage
T The hut housing the machine for lowering enthroned gods, etc., to the stage
U The 'Heavens'
W Hoisting the playhouse flag

# Part 1

# Introduction

## William Shakespeare

The eldest son of a prosperous glover, William Shakespeare was born in April 1564 in Stratford-upon-Avon in Warwickshire. His father, who also dealt in timber and wool, was well respected, being elected Bailiff and in 1571 Chief Alderman of the town.

William Shakespeare received his free education at the King's New School in Stratford, set up by charter in 1553. There he spent long hours learning axioms and Latin authors such as Virgil (70–19BC), Horace (65–8BC), Cicero (106–43BC) and Caesar (102–44BC).

During his teens, he exercised his father's trade. When he was 18, he got Anne Hathaway (eight years his senior) with child. This led to their hurried marriage in late November 1582. For the next seven years no records exist. Conjecture has it that Shakespeare became a schoolmaster in Warwickshire, that he was prosecuted for deer-stealing, that he was forced to leave the county of Warwickshire and shelter in London. It is likely that in the summer of 1587 he joined a touring company of actors and later accompanied them to London.

By 1592, competing against the young wits of the universities, who had until then monopolised play-writing, Shakespeare attracted London audiences with *Henry VI, Love's Labour's Lost, The Comedy of Errors*, and the *Taming of the Shrew*.

During the plague years 1592 to 1594, Shakespeare wrote and dedicated to Henry Wriothesley, third Earl of Southampton, the narrative poems *Venus and Adonis* and *The Rape of Lucrece*. Southampton became his friend and patron, and soon, apparently, successful rival in love for the mysterious Dark Lady of the Sonnets, with whom Shakespeare seems to have been violently in love.

In 1594, Shakespeare acquired a player's share in the Lord Chamberlain's Company, later renamed The King's Men. By this time many of the established playwrights—Christopher Marlowe (1564–93), Robert Greene (1558–92) and Thomas Kyd (1558–94)—were dead, and Shakespeare was consolidating his reputation with *Romeo and Juliet* and *The Merchant of Venice*. This brought considerable financial reward, and when in 1598 The Theatre playhouse was dismantled and the timber used to build The Globe, Shakespeare acquired a right to ten per cent of the profits.

The years 1601–2 were particularly galling. Shakespeare's friends, Robert Devereux, Earl of Essex (1566–1601), and Henry Wriothesley, Earl of Southampton (1573–1624), stimulated political unrest and Queen Elizabeth's reign drew to a bitter close. After the execution of Essex for treason, and the imprisonment of Southampton, Shakespeare wrote *Troilus and Cressida*.

To this period belong the other 'problem' plays, *All's Well* and *Measure for Measure*—all leaving the audience with an unpleasant taste in the mouth. The great tragedies followed, and Shakespeare's greatness was established for ever.

Meanwhile Shakespeare had acquired considerable estate in Stratford. In 1597 he purchased New Place, which became his permanent residence after 1611. There on 23 April 1616, at the age of 52, Shakespeare died of a fever, allegedly after a merry drinking bout with the writers Michael Drayton (1563–1631) and Ben Jonson (1572–1637).

# The Elizabethan theatre and conventions

If, as is probable, Shakespeare joined a company of actors on tour in the provinces sometime in 1587, he must have had to put up with bad roads, uncomfortable beds, and improvised theatres at public inn-yard or market cross.

In London, conditions were markedly better. Besides private theatres, guildhalls, Inns of Court, and the halls of Royal Palaces, there were public playhouses—the Theatre, the Curtain, the Rose, and the Swan. Of the latter we possess the De Witt sketch which, together with the building contracts for the Fortune and Hope playhouses, provides a comprehensive framework of the Elizabethan multiple stage: a roughly circular galleried auditorium, a raised, partly roofed, stage, supported by massive Corinthian posts, two double-hung 2½-metre (7-ft) doors at the back; behind these was the 'tiring house', *mimorum aedes*; and a balcony. Modelled on and developed from the public inn-yards of the period, the public playhouses (the first of which, the Theatre, was built in 1576) differed substantially from private theatres, so beloved of Elizabethan actors.

Except for the Fortune, public playhouses were all 'round', roughly octagonal. They were three-storeyed, with multiple acting areas, were unroofed, open to the weather, and a flag flew from the turret when a play was on. They had no lighting facilities, depending exclusively on daylight and except for the scenic wall, they had no painted scenery. The playhouses were large, accommodating up to 3,000 spectators, the majority standing.

Raised about 1·35 metres (4 ft 6 in) and gently sloping, the stage jutted out into the middle of the pit, and was surrounded by three tiers of galleries and the penny-paying 'groundlings' on three sides. The stage of the Fortune was 8·1 metres (27 ft) deep and, at its widest, 12·9 metres (43 ft) wide. It must have been considerably narrower in the 'round' playhouses.

In the middle there was a trap-door, leading down to the cellar or 'hell' underlying the whole stage. There was another trap-door backstage.

At the back, at first-floor level, there was the dressing-room or 'tiring house', where actors waited for their cue, and where magnificent costumes were at the ready. This led on to the 'tarras' or balcony. It has often been suggested that at ground-level there must have been an 'inner' proscenium arch stage about 2·4 metres by 6·9 metres (8 ft by 27 ft), but this theory is now generally discarded in favour of the curtained 0·6 metres (2 ft) deep 'discovery space'.

Some Elizabethan dramatic conventions seem artificial:

(i) The plays lacked intervals.

(ii) They were often written in blank verse, with rhyming couplets marking the end of the scene.

(iii) Female parts, such as those of Cressida or Cassandra, were acted by boys with unbroken voices.

(iv) If a character assumed a disguise, it was impenetrable even to close friends.

(v) If an actor stepped forward to deliver an 'Aside', fellow-actors would not hear him

(vi) A character could speak out most secret thoughts in soliloquy to the audience.

(vii) There being no front curtains, 'dead' bodies had to be carried off the stage at the end of the scene.

(viii) As there was hardly any scenery between the actor's 'stretched footing and the scaffoldage' (*Troilus and Cressida*, I.3.156), the bare boards subsequently represented widely differing locations—Priam's Palace, a Trojan street, a Greek camp, Pandarus's orchard, Achilles's tent, a battlefield.

It is necessary, therefore, that in performance the main geographical locations be clearly established. Thus, for example, a director will decide that the balcony is Cressida's room; that under the balcony is Priam's court; that the middle stage is the Greek camp; that the forestage is neutral, the distinction between Greek and Trojan being maintained by dressing one group in Elizabethan, and the other in Classical, costume. When such conventions are accepted, the play can be performed successfully, without unnecessary breaks.

# The Elizabethan world order

Hector's insistence on the right of the community to control the individual's appetite (II.2.173ff.) reinforces Ulysses's justifiably famous speech on degree and *correspondences* in a universe threatened by appetite. That there is a gap between what the two men say and what they do constitutes one of the main ironies of the play.

In many of his plays, Shakespeare maintained that unrest and civil strife are not only bad in themselves but are reflected in nature, and lead to cosmic disorder. Thus in *Macbeth* horses turn carnivorous soon after the murder of the king; in *Julius Caesar* 'the heavens themselves declare the death of princes'; in *King Lear* the King's self-consuming rage is reflected in the wild storm; in *Troilus and Cressida* Ulysses argues that even planets wander in disorder when the 'specialty of rule' is not respected.

Despite the growing influence of *Il Principe* [The Prince] (1514) by the Italian Nicolo Macchiavelli (1469–1527) which stressed aspiration and the will to power, many Elizabethans still found comfort in the existence of a great chain of being that stretched down from God to the meanest inanimate object, and up again through the several classes of being—elements, vegetation, beasts, man, angels.

Each class had its own primate or leader, first in rank and authority—as gold, lion, eagle, sun and King. Everything in the universe contributed towards the development or well-being of other species. Man was central, the perfection of earth's generative action, and human events had repercussions all along the chain.

A King was paramount among men and he derived his power from God. Aided from above, and supported by the various ranks below him, a king held together the social and political fabric established by God and nature. Disharmony and chaos resulted when a king relinquished his responsibilities, or when 'degree is suffocate' through civil disobedience.

These ideas formed part of a collective belief which studied strife against the traditional world view inherited from the Middle Ages, still supported by the official Tudor doctrine on obedience.

Ulysses's celebrated speech draws on several well-known sources.

Among these is *The Boke of the Governour* (1531) by Thomas Elyot (1499?–1546):

> Take away order from all things. What should then remain? Certainly nothing finally, except some man would imagine immediate chaos . . . where there is any lack of order there must needs be perpetual conflict . . .

Elizabethan sermons on the obedience of the subject also stressed the upholding of order through rank. Thus the *First Book of Homilies* (1547):

> Take away kings, princes, rulers, magistrates, judges and such estates of God's order, no man shall ride or go by the highway unrobbed; no man shall sleep in his own house or bed unkilled.

Nearer to Shakespeare's play, we find *Of the Laws of Ecclesiastical Polity* (1594) by Richard Hooker (1554–1600):

> If the frame of that heavenly arch erected over our heads should loosen and dissolve itself; if celestial spheres should forget their wonted motions . . . what would become of man himself, whom these things now do all serve?

This is exactly what Troilus believes after witnessing Cressida's betrayal: 'The bonds of heaven are slipped, dissolved and loosed.' (V.2.151–3)

## Shakespeare and the sources

Some features relating to the siege of Troy (*c.*1240BC), particularly the rape of Helen, the wrath of Achilles, and the slaying of Hector, were widely popular in Shakespeare's time. The legend of Troy owed its popularity to Virgil's *Aeneid*, Ovid's *Metamorphoses*, and to Homer's *Iliad*. In England, immediately prior to *Troilus and Cressida*, a series of works elaborated the 'historical' matter of Troy and overlaid it with fantastic additions—political, moral and romantic. Among these we can mention *Euphues, His Censure to Philautus* (1587) by Robert Greene (1558–92), *The Tale of Troy* (1589) by George Peele (1558–97), and the play *troyless and creseda* (1599) by Henry Chettle (d. 1607) and Thomas Dekker (1570–1632). But there were other sources. *Ephemeris Belli Troiani* by Dictys Cretensis, reputed author of an eye-witness account of the Trojan war, was supposedly discovered during the Emperor Nero's reign (AD54–68) and translated into Latin prose in the fourth century. This diary branded the Trojans as rash and irresponsible, questioned their chivalry, and described Hector as 'a wolf

Ravishing and Insatiable'. In contrast, the pro-Trojan *De Excidio Troiae Historiae* by Dares of Phrygia, reputed author of a rival eyewitness account, translated into Latin in the fifth century, challenged Dicty's account, castigated the Greeks, and became the authoritative source.

The love-story of Troilus and Cressida was first recounted at length in *Le Roman de Troie* (1160) by the troubadour Benoit de Sainte Maure (flourished *c*.1155–75). This describes Troilus's love tryst and his infatuation, Cressida's leave-taking, Diomed's wooing and the growing hatred between Diomed and Troilus. Translated into Italian as *Historia Troiana* (1287) by Guido delle Colonne (*c*.1243–89), this became the chief source for many verse and prose works, the best known of which is *Il Filostrato* (1335) by Giovanni Boccaccio (1313–75) who developed the story into a full romance. This influenced *Troilus and Criseyde* (1386 ?) by Geoffrey Chaucer (1340–1400), and this in turn influenced Shakespeare's play.

It has often been maintained that elements in Shakespeare's love-plot are borrowed from Chaucer. Thus the scene where Pandarus sings the praises of Troilus (I.2.183ff.) seems derived from the passage in *Troilus and Criseyde* where Criseyde watches Troilus's return from battle amid Trojan shouts of jubilation (Bk.II.610–51); that Troilus's apprehension and confusion on his first meeting Cressida (III.2.17ff.) is similar to Chaucer's (Bk.II.1751–57); that Cressida's vow of loyalty (IV.2.106) and her hypocrisy in sending a letter of reassurance (V.3.108ff.) derive from Chaucer (Bks.IV.1534–54; V.1590ff.).

Another source was the *Troy-Book* (1412), later published as *The Hystorye Siege and Dystruccyon of Troye* (1513), by John Lydgate (1370?–1450), who paints the Trojans as immensely chivalric. From Lydgate, Shakespeare probably borrowed Ulysses's thumb-nail sketch of Troilus (IV.5.95–112); Hector's rash hunting of the knight in sumptuous armour (V.6 and 8); and Achilles's treacherous instructions to the Myrmidons (V.7).

From the *Recuyell of the Historyes of Troye* (1474), printed by William Caxton (*c*.1422–91), the first English printer, Shakespeare derived material for the description of Priam's Troy and the city gates in the Prologue, Cressida's welcome by the Greek generals, Achilles's insolence (IV.5.229–50) towards Hector, Agamemnon's roll call of victors and victims (V.5.6–15), and the tying of Hector's body to the horse's tail. The last incident is also found in Lydgate.

*Seaven Bookes of the Iliades* (1598) by George Chapman (1559?–1634) provided a direct translation from Homer. It is probable that the challenge to single combat and its acceptance by Ajax, Achilles's insubordination, Achilles's friendship with Patroclus and the decision to return to battle, Ulysses's analysis of Greek division, the reference to the gods taking sides in the war were inspired by Chapman's version.

Shakespeare used these sources creatively. He twisted out of shape the courtly love conventions of Chaucer, mocked the elements of hero-worship predominant in the works of his contemporaries, and deflated the 'Achillean' virtues proclaimed in the Preface to Chapman's Homer. Modifying the tone, incident and motive of his sources, Shakespeare deliberately flouted accepted tradition. He punctured lofty idealism with scurrility and cynicism, mingled noble sentiment with bawdy, tragedy with downright burlesque.

# A note on the text

Since 1557, authorship and 'copyright' were claimed by entering a book or play for publication in the Stationers' Register. *Troilus and Cressida* was entered twice. The first conditional 'holding' entry for 1603 reads:

> *7 Februarii. Master Robertes. Entred for his copie in full Court holden this day to print when he hath gotten sufficient aucthority for yt. The booke of Troilus and Cresseda as yt is acted by my lord Chamberlens Men.*

Nothing came of this and the play was not printed. A second entry for 1609 reads:

> *28 Januarii. Richard Bonion Henry Walleys. Entred for their Copy under thandes of Master Segar deputy to Sir George Bucke and master warden Lownes a booke called the history of Troylus and Cressida.*

Printing started almost immediately. The original 1609 Quarto title-page reads:

> *The / Historie of Troylus / and Cresseida / As it was acted by the Kings Maiesties / servants at the Globe / Written by William Shakespeare.*

This was cancelled and replaced by a new title-page, omitting the reference to a Globe performance:

> *The / Famous Historie of / Troylus and Cresseid. / Excellently expressing the beginning / of their loves, with the conceited wooing / of Pandarus Prince of Licia. / Written by William Shakespeare.*

This also included a Publisher's Epistle flatly contradicting the original title page. It said that the play was never before performed on a public stage: 'never stal'd with the stage, never clapper-clawd with the palmes of the vulgar ... the smoaky breath of the multitude'; that the play is a comedy: 'passing full of the palme comicall ... none more witty than this.'

However, the 1609 Quarto title-pages describe it as a 'Historie', while the 1623 Folio, which alone contains the Prologue, calls it a 'Tragedie'.

The overall satiric tone of the play has prompted critics to suggest that it was originally intended for a sophisticated private audience, or that the cynical Pandarus's 'epilogue' was an afterthought inserted for the unshockable benchers, barristers and law students at the Inns of Court. The textual evidence for this is scanty and insufficient.

All quotations in these Notes refer to the edition in the New Cambridge Shakespeare, *Troilus and Cressida* edited by Alice Walker, Cambridge University Press, Cambridge, 1954.

# Part 2

# Summaries
*of* TROILUS AND CRESSIDA

## A general summary

Frustrated love for fair Cressida distracts Troilus from the Trojan war effort. He sees her as a model of virtue, so 'stubborn chaste' as to be almost beyond him. She is really a calculating coquette who revels in bawdy talk. Troilus's main hope lies in the go-between Pandarus, Cressida's uncle and protector who praises Troilus as 'prince of chivalry'.

This dawning romance is set against the cloying love of Paris for the beautiful Helen, stolen in retaliation from the Greek Menelaus, for whose wounded pride and honour the Greeks have besieged Troy for seven years. Things have reached an impasse. Ulysses explains how petty rivalries and disrespect for a central authority have weakened the Greek forces and prevented a total victory: 'Troy in our weakness lives, not in her strength.'

The zest and valour of Achilles have turned to pride. Disgruntled, Achilles sulks in his tent, pouring scorn on Agamemnon's insufficiency and the 'closet war' of his advisors. He idles his hours away, encouraging the effeminate Patroclus to mimic the mental and physical failings of his superiors. Self-sufficient and 'possessed with greatness', Achilles totally abandons the Greek war effort. Since his withdrawal, a heroic epic war has been reduced to paltry 'pelting' skirmishes. This military inaction has bred division in the camp. War-weariness and dissension have suppressed the original impetus and marred all pretence to chivalry. This is reflected in Thersites's jibe that the whole argument is 'a cuckold and a whore'.

Events come to a head when Aeneas interrupts the Greek council debate to deliver Hector's valiant challenge to single combat. Ulysses grasps this opportunity, prompts the Greeks to fake a lottery and 'by design' to select the boorish Ajax as new Greek champion. They vainly hope that this slight or rejection of Achilles would sting him into action.

Meanwhile the Trojans debate a Greek message to surrender Helen in return for lifting the siege. As a responsible leader, Hector argues that too many lives have been sacrificed for an idea—Helen is 'not worth what she doth cost the holding.' Paris and Troilus insist that Helen is a 'theme of honour and renown' not to be surrendered on terms of 'base compulsion'. The prophetess Cassandra foretells the sack of Troy unless they 'let Helen go'.

Unexpectedly, Hector makes what seems to be a mental somersault. He abandons the 'way of truth' and, agreeing with Troilus, votes for the continued defence of Helen as reflecting on their 'joint and several dignities'. He surprises the council by informing them of his challenge already delivered to the Greeks.

Meanwhile, through Pandarus's good services, Troilus and Cressida are brought together. They swear eternal love to each other, but Cressida's oath of constancy anticipates her future duplicity: 'Yea let them say to stick the heart of falsehood/As false as Cressid'. They go in and consummate their love.

Immediately things take an ugly turn. Cressida's father, the renegade seer Calchas who has deserted Troy, requests Agamemnon to 'buy' Cressida in exchange for the Trojan strategist Antenor who had just been taken prisoner.

When the Trojan council agree to this request, Troilus is still secretly making love to Cressida, and later he has to submit to the general decision. The demands of war take precedence over love, and Cressida must join her father behind the Greek lines. Determined that he will 'grow friend with danger', Troilus promises Cressida he will visit her nightly. Cressida seems genuinely moved and distressed by this sudden blow of fate, and exchanges her glove for Troilus's 'sleeve' as a pledge of her constancy. However, during the angry flare-up between Troilus and the Greek envoy Diomed, Cressida remains curiously silent, sizing up the situation. By the time she crosses over to the Greeks, she has shifted her allegiance. Determined to be a survivor, she quickly adopts Diomed as her 'sweet guardian'. The kissing-test anticipates her fickleness, and Ulysses proclaims her a wanton 'daughter of the game'.

The single combat between Hector and Ajax turns out to be a tame bloodless affair, marked by chivalry and courtesy on both sides, except for the insolence of Achilles: 'Tell me ye heavens, in which part of his body shall I destroy him.' But an unquiet truce is proclaimed, and Achilles promises to engage Hector in battle: 'Tomorrow do I meet thee, fell as death.' This is followed by Greek hospitality, feasting, drinking and celebrations. Achilles's bloodthirstiness becomes evident. Only a message from the Trojan princess Polyxena, with whom he is deeply in love, makes him decide against going to war: 'Fall Greeks, fail fame . . . My major vow lies here; this I'll obey.' (V.1.42–3)

Meanwhile Diomed claims his right to Cressida: 'they say he keeps a Trojan drab and uses the traitor Calchas's tent.' In a scene of visual originality, Ulysses, Troilus and the scurrilous Thersites are witness to

Cressida's surrender of her 'sweet, sweet sleeve'. At first Troilus will not believe his eyes, 'This is and is not Cressida', but then his whole world collapses at his feet. Disillusioned, he returns to Troy vowing 'venom'd vengeance' and raging against Hector's fair play in battle.

The next morning, hedged in by Cassandra's prophecies of doom, Hector and Troilus go to battle, doing 'mad and fantastic execution'. Patroclus is slain, and this stings Achilles into action. His continued inaction makes him no match for a fitter Hector. He is easily winded and it is only Hector's 'vice of mercy' that spares his life. The despicable Achilles then instructs his Myrmidons in treachery and effects the planned gang-murder of Hector. He desecrates Hector's body by tying it to his horse's tail and dragging it around the city walls.

This seems to anticipate the fall of Troy, and even Troilus begs the gods not to linger 'our sure destructions on'. The only comfort Troilus can offer his armies is that of revenge.

When Pandarus, his friend and go-between, incongruously appears on the battle-scene, an embittered Troilus dismisses him with a curse: 'Ignomy and shame pursue thy life'. Pandarus, who is just as disillusioned, tries to shrug off this dismissal by launching his own satiric attack on the audience's sensibility.

# Detailed summaries

## Prologue

The Prologue sets the scene for the burning and plunder of Troy by the Greeks. No mention is made of Troilus and Cressida who lend their names to the title of the play.

The emphasis is on epic deeds and the excitement of battle. However, the grandiose language (**princes orgulous, warlike fraughtage**) and heroic action are undercut by blunt dismissive scorn—Helen sleeps with wanton Paris, 'and that's the quarrel'.

This early deflation sets the tone for the frequent statements that these long ruinous wars and lengthy philosophical debates have centred on objects of little worth.

NOTES AND GLOSSARY
**princes orgulous ... chafed:** angered arrogant princes
**Phrygia:** district in Western Asia Minor, of which Troy was the capital
**Tenedos:** a small island, used as port by the Greeks during the siege of Troy

**warlike fraughtage:** cargo, freight. In this case, soldiers
**Dardan:** Trojan
**Priam's six-gated city ... Antenorides:** these gates are not mentioned in Homer's *Iliad*, but in Caxton's *Recuyell of the Hystoryes of Troye*
**corresponsive and fulfilling:** exactly-fitting
**sperr up:** securely shut
**prologue armed but not in confidence ... argument:** the prologue usually wore a black cloak. In this case it is an armed combatant who speaks. This refers to Ben Jonson's play, *Poetaster* (1601) which had a 'prologue armed in well erected confidence' against the writer's critics. This links *Troilus and Cressida* with the 'war of the theatres' which involved the dramatists Ben Jonson (1572–1637), John Marston (1575–1634) and Thomas Dekker (1570–1632)
**vaunt broils:** beginning of those wars

---

**Act I Scene 1:** *Troy—before Priam's palace*

---

This opening is in the mock-heroic mode, setting the play on its satiric course. Love-sick Troilus hampers the Trojan war aims by his great love for Cressida. Troilus wants to unarm again. Frustrated, he quarrels with his go-between who urges patience.

Pandarus compares the wooing of Cressida to baking a cake that must be eaten and consumed. This 'low' imagery mocks the idealism of the Court and is in contrast to the traditional imagery (broken heart, cygnet's down, drowned hopes) used by Troilus. However, Troilus is realistic about Helen of Troy's worth. She is 'too starved a subject' for his sword, and those who engage in futile wars 'Fools on both sides'. On the other hand, the mental image that immediately follows is that of Cressida's beauty and worth—romantic, inflated and highly-idealised. Her beauty is an index of her moral worth. She is virtuous and 'stubborn-chaste', and in his over-wrought emotional state, Troilus speaks of himself as the merchant adventuring across the wild seas in search of an Indian pearl.

The entry of Aeneas brings him back to reality, and Troilus reluctantly goes to battle!

NOTES AND GLOSSARY
**Will this gear ne'er be mended?:** Will this fuss and bother never end?
**meddle nor make:** interfere any more in the wooing of Cressida

**bolting:** sifting, passed through a sieve

**Patience herself . . .than I do:** Patience herself is not more patient than I

**So, traitor! . . . When is she thence?:** Troilus accuses himself of treachery for suggesting that Cressida could ever be absent from his thoughts

**wedged . . . rive in twain:** split with a sigh, would break in two

**Cassandra's wit:** the gift of prophecy

**spirit of sense:** sense of touch

**she has the mends:** she can find her own remedy

**as fair o' Friday . . . Sunday:** Cressida is fairer than Helen any day

**stay behind her father:** Calchas went to Delphi to consult the oracle. Learning that the Trojans would be defeated he deserted to the Greeks

**Apollo for thy Daphne's love:** Daphne, the nymph, changed into a bay tree to escape the god Apollo's chase

**Ilium:** Priam's Palace

**this woman's answer sorts:** my excuse would have been more appropriate if given by a woman

**scar to scorn . . . Menelaus' horn:** a slight wound deserving of scorn, considering Paris was gored by the cuckold's horn he gave Menelaus

**Better at home . . . may:** I would prefer to make love to Cressida but . . .

---

**Act I Scene 2:** *a street in Troy*

---

This scene, remarkable for its indecent word-play by Cressida, strongly reinforces the elements mocking the grand epic manner and courtly love tradition. In the previous scene we saw Cressida through Troilus's eyes. The point of view now shifts.

The scene begins earnestly enough. Hector, the great Trojan hero, is reported shamed and visibly annoyed. He had earlier been wounded by the Greek warrior Ajax. In reaction, Hector chides his wife, strikes his armourer and goes to battle in anger. There is a promise of impending heroic action.

However, as soon as Cressida speaks the mocking process starts again. Her fondness for bawdy talk suggests she is not the 'stubborn-chaste' that Troilus imagined. She actually strives to be witty, punning at every opportunity, effectively debunking her uncle Pandar who recommends Troilus in real earnest. Pandar argues Troilus is 'a better man' than Hector. Cressida not only makes fun of the prowess of Pandar's prince of chivalry, but the numerous sexual innuendos destroy Troilus's idealistic image of Cressida as the virtuous fair.

Although Cressida is aware that she must guard her reputation, her frequent indecent word-play suggests she is ripe for the picking: 'upon my back to defend my belly ... unless it swell past hiding.'

Cressida's shift to verse in the soliloquy 'Words, vows ...' is not enough to lift the tone of the scene. Although she claims to see more in Troilus 'than in the glass of Pandar's praise may be', her trite sentential couplets stress the reduction or cutting down to size of Troilus's image. Cressida's 'firm love' sounds hollow and the audience is struck rather by her self-love and cool calculation.

NOTES AND GLOSSARY

**a very man per se:** unique

**particular additions:** individual characteristics

**crowded humours:** contradictory traits and attitudes. In mediæval physiology the 'humours' referred to the four fluids (black bile, blood, phlegm, yellow bile) found in the constitution of the body. Their relative proportions determined a person's health and temperament

**attaint:** defect

**against the hair:** irritably

**Briareus:** a monster with a hundred hands in Greek mythology

**Argus:** in Greek mythology a herdsman with eyes covering his body

**coped:** encountered, engaged in battle

**he'll lay about him:** he'll leave destruction behind

**Condition ... barefoot to India:** even if I had to go barefoot to India to restore Troilus to his usual self

**come to't:** reached maturity

**brown favour:** dark complexion

**copper nose:** infirmity causing extreme redness of face

**merry Greek:** frivolous, irresponsible person

**compassed window:** bay window

**tapster's arithmetic:** elementary counting or reckoning

**so old a lifter:** so experienced a thief; the context suggests *limb-lifter*, or fornicator

**stand to the proof:** a bawdy pun relating to sexual arousal

**addle:** rotten

**rack:** torture

**with millstones:** excessive mirth and laughter

**Marry:** an oath, 'By the Virgin Mary'

**two and fifty:** Priam had fifty sons. Since the white hair stands for Priam, and Paris's 'forked hair' counts for two, they add up to fifty-two

**forked:** referring to the cuckold's horns. Paris had cuckolded Menelaus

**told you a thing yesterday:** referring to Troilus's love suit

**Will he give you the nod? ... have more:** refers to the card name called 'noddy'. Cressida means that Pandarus will become a bigger fool

**there's laying on ... who will:** no one can deny the evidence of strong blows exchanged

**a grace:** attendant goddess

**drayman ... camel:** fit for carrying loads

**no date in the pie:** pies seasoned with dates were thought to be an aphrodisiac, or sexual stimulant

**the man's date is out:** he has uncovered himself, naked

**at what ward you lie:** technical expression used in fencing or swordplay

**honesty:** chastity

**unless it swell past hiding:** unless I become pregnant

**bawd:** procurer; trader in sex

**That she:** woman

**Achievement is command; ungained, beseech:** when men win a woman they command her; while still trying to win her, they must beg

---

**Act I Scene 3:** *the Greek camp, before Agamemnon's tent*

---

This scene which, together with II.2, forms the philosophical centre of the play moves to a Greek Council discussing the failure to take Troy after seven years' siege. Agamemnon and Nestor ascribe this to chance and the 'protractive trials of great Jove' who seeks to test their endurance. Ulysses, however, in his famous speech on order and degree (II.3.75–137) argues that factions have been allowed to stray from the social and political power of Agamemnon. Once 'the specialty of rule' is neglected, moral rot sets in allowing appetite and self-indulgence to control reason. This leads to discord, failure to distinguish between right and wrong, and a general chaos that threatens dissolution.

Ulysses blames Achilles who sulks in his tent with the effeminate Patroclus, mocking the war problems of the Greeks. It is this general disrespect towards authority that is breeding division. This is often spoken of in terms of disease and fever. Despite the sublime comparisons between the King and the sun's 'medicinable eye', Agamemnon's inefficiency is exposed when the Trojan Aeneas interrupts the Greek Council's deliberations and does not recognise Agamemnon. Visibly annoyed, Agamemnon asserts his authority and in so doing emphasises he is no 'god in office' guiding men.

Aeneas delivers a challenge obviously directed at Achilles, but Ulysses has a 'young conception in my brain'. He is to fake a lottery and 'by device, the blockish Ajax' will be the Greek choice to engage Hector in single combat. Whether Ajax wins or not, Achilles's pride will be hurt. There is then an obvious gap between words and deeds, between the earlier magnificent speeches about unity and degree and the present trickery behind apparently heroic actions.

NOTES AND GLOSSARY

| | |
|---|---|
| **Sennet:** | trumpet call |
| **jaundice:** | disease causing yellowing of skin and eyes |
| **tortive and errant:** | twisted, without control |
| **Sith every action . . . shape:** | projects such as ours have often failed |
| **affined and kin:** | related, similar |
| **bauble boats:** | toy boats |
| **Boreas . . . Thetis:** | the North Wind starts a sea storm |
| **Perseus's horse:** | Pegasus, the winged horse, more often associated with Bellerophon in Greek mythology |
| **a toast for Neptune:** | a victim for the Roman sea-god |
| **breese:** | gadfly |
| **high in brass . . . silver:** | Agamemnon's speech, like public records of important events, deserves to be engraved in brass, and Nestor's in silver. But compare I.3.296 for Nestor's 'silver beard' |
| **mastic:** | gummy |
| **The specialty of rule:** | obligation in accepting power of authority |
| **When that the general . . . honey is expected?:** | When the general does not act like a strong centre of refuge and sustenance success will not crown the enterprise |
| **Degree being vizarded . . . mask:** | when the contract to accept authority and precedence is not observed, real worth cannot be distinguished |
| **the glorious planet sol:** | despite growing support for Nicholas Copernicus (1473–1543), many believed that the earth was still at the centre of the universe |
| **Corrects . . . planets evil:** | in astrology, planetary influence varied with the sun's change of position with respect to other planets |
| **deracinate:** | uproot |
| **primogenitive:** | under English law, the right of the eldest son to inherit all the real estate |

**mere oppugnancy:** total discord and strife

**Strength should be lord of imbecility:** the strong would dominate the weak and unprotected

**bloodless emulation:** weakening rivalry and envy

**The sinew and the forehand of our host:** foremost warrior in our army

**Grows dainty:** finicky and demanding

**pageants:** mimics, makes fun of

**topless deputation:** sovereign unlimited rights

**whose conceit lies in his hamstring:** whose understanding lies in the tendon of his leg

**o'erwrested seeming:** forced unsuccessful attempt at imitation

**rearing Typhon:** monster with serpent heads, father of hurricane winds

**As like as Vulcan and his wife:** very unlike. In Greek mythology Haephaestos (Vulcan) was the God of fire and metal working. Ugly and sooty, he married Aphrodite (Venus) the beautiful Goddess of erotic love

**gorget:** throat armour

**paradoxes:** absurdities, curiosities, oddities

**Forestall prescience:** discount and perhaps hinder foresight

**So that the ram . . . guide his execution:** they consider the battering ram more important than the engineer who devised it

**Achilles' horse make many Thetis' sons:** if this were true, Achilles's horse may be worth as much as Achilles and his Myrmidons

**when she coldly eyes the youthful Phoebus:** when I see the rising sun. This refers back to I.3.89–94 which compared Agamemnon to the sun

**to set his sense on the attentive bent:** to make him listen with attention

**long-continued truce:** This implies a considerable lapse of time between I.2 and I.3

**That loves his mistress . . . arms than hers:** who, by accepting the challenge, is prepared to prove in deed that his vows are not idle

**The Grecian dames are sunburnt . . . lance:** blemished, not worth defending

**bearer . . . vantbrace:** moveable face guard in helmet . . . armour that protects the forearm

**heavens forfend such scarcity of youth:** heavens forbid that no young warrior should take up the challenge

**I have a young conception . . . shape:** I have an idea which you might help to develop

**the purpose is perspicuous ... sum up:** what is really behind this
challenge is made clear by little hints
**taste ... fin'st palate:** match our best warrior with theirs
**Our imputation ... wild action:** our reputation may be at risk in this
irresponsible encounter
**scantling:** indication, or foretaste
**our main opinion crush ... our best man:** undermine our reputation if
our best man is defeated
**physic the great Myrmidon:** hurt Achilles's pride
**crest that prouder than blue Iris bends:** like the rainbow, the pride of
Achilles reaches for the heavens. In Homer's epic,
the *Iliad*, she carried messages for the Gods. She
was originally a personification of the rainbow
**pride alone ... their bone:** Achilles and Ajax are provoked to fight for
glory, as dogs quarrel over a bone

---

**Act II Scene 1:** *the Greek camp*

---

In the previous scene, Agamemnon was compared to the Sun whose
'medicinable eye' corrects evil influences. He was also the 'nerve and
bone of Greece' and therefore his condition was indicative of the well-
being of the army. But dissension has become so rife that Agamemnon's
failure to assert his authority results in his being infected as well.

Thersites, who acts as an anti-Greek chorus, speaks of Agamemnon
as a 'botchy core', an erupted boil or tumour. The disease is now more
fully developed in recurrent imagery of a running sore infecting the
whole army.

The scene ridicules the choice of 'blockish Ajax' as the Greek
champion. Ajax and Achilles are accused of allowing themselves to be
used to 'plough up the wars'.

Towards the end Achilles is visibly annoyed at having to inform Ajax
what the rigged lottery is all about.

NOTES AND GLOSSARY

**matter:** substance and direction; also pus erupting from sore
or boil
**mongrel:** Ajax was half Trojan and half Greek
**vinewed'st leaven:** most mildewed bread
**without book:** by heart
**red murrain:** plague sores
**porpentine:** porcupine, or hedgehog
**forth in the incursions:** engaged in battle

**Cerberus is at Proserpina's beauty:** a three-headed dog guarded the entrance to the underworld. In Greek mythology Proserpina (Persephone, daughter of the Earth Goddess Demeter) was carried off by the God of the Underworld, Pluto. The Earth then refused to bear fruit until Pluto allowed Proserpina to return for eight months of the year. Her return to earth and the consequent sproutings of crops in the spring was celebrated in many rituals

**stool for a witch:** method of torture
**assinego:** ass, fool
**bought and sold:** ridiculed, made fun of
**pia mater:** brain
**impress:** with reference to compulsory military service
**fusty:** mouldy
**to, Achilles! to, Ajax, to:** shouts of a farmer urging oxen forward
**brach:** bitch
**clotpolls:** fools, and blockheads
**the fifth hour:** eleven o'clock
**that hath a stomach:** who feels like fighting

---

**Act II Scene 2:** *Troy—Priam's palace*

---

You need to read this scene very carefully and compare it to the Greek Council in I.3. The scene is philosophically complex.

After reading Nestor's message demanding Helen, Priam specifically asks Hector's advice. The bravest of the Trojans urges prudence, and argues that Helen 'is not worth' the Trojan lives that have been sacrificed for her. Reason suggests she ought to be surrendered to the Greeks.

Speaking against crammed Reason, Troilus argues that worth or value is not absolute, but relative. Earlier it had seemed to Troilus that Helen was 'too starved' a subject for his sword. Now she is reassessed, and, like Cressida, becomes a pearl of inestimable value. It would therefore be cowardice to yield her up.

At this stage enters Cassandra, declaring and anticipating the doom that controls the rest of the action: 'Cry, cry! Troy burns, or else let Helen go'. Despite this, Troilus and Paris argue that they should battle on to defend Helen, and their 'several honours'.

This is where Hector takes up the theme of order and appetite. He explores the root of sin and the necessity to distinguish between right and wrong. The laws of nature demand that husbands have a moral claim on their wives. Men refuse to accept this because passion prevails against reason. However, nations have established laws to control those 'appetites that are most disobedient.' Helen must be returned.

At this stage, however, Hector makes a complete turn that has puzzled commentators. Seeing the truth, he 'nevertheless' moves away towards the defence of their 'joint and several dignities'. He informs the Trojans that he has sent a challenge to the Greeks which must wake them to their responsibility.

NOTES AND GLOSSARY

**consumed ... cormorant war:** wasted in this ruinous gluttonous war

**touches my particular:** concerns me personally

**more softer bowels:** more against violence

**The wound of peace is surety:** peace is destroyed by a false sense of security

**tent ... worst:** absorbent lint that cleans the worst wound

**Every tithe soul ... as dear as Helen:** every soldier sacrificed has been as dear as Helen

**counters sum up ... infinite?:** will you compare the King's infinite merit with worthless bits of metal?

**You fur your gloves with reason:** reason provides you with a comfortable excuse

**chidden Mercury:** Mercury was the Roman God of merchants, early identified with the Greek God Hermes, herald and messenger of the Gods. Jove (Jupiter) Chief God of the Romans was often identified with the Greek God Zeus

**star disorbed:** shooting star

**crammed reason:** filled to excess

**makes livers pale and lustihood deject:** make men lose courage and manliness fail

**But value dwells not ... affected merit:** merit is not a matter of opinion. To be really worth anything an object must be valuable of itself, and must be recognised as such by others. Only a corrupted will prizes an object of no value

**remainder viands ... unrespective sieve:** we do not throw the rest of the food in refuse baskets

**an old aunt:** Hesione, Priam's sister and Ajax's mother, who was held captive by Telamon, King of Salamis

**hath launched above a thousand ships:** with reference to Marlowe's *Dr Faustus* (V.1.107): 'Was this the face that launched a thousand ships?'

**the issue ... wisdoms rate:** scorn your previous decisions

**beggar the estimation:** make value-less what you previously esteemed so highly

**a moiety ... moan to come:** a part of our future suffering

**our firebrand brother:** when Hecuba was pregnant with Paris, she dreamed she was delivered of a flaming torch

**the world convince of levity:** opinion convict us of irresponsibility

**gave wings to my propension:** supported my inclination and desire

**besotted:** stupefied or intoxicated

**on terms of base compulsion:** forced into yielding

**glozed:** commented

**Aristotle:** an obvious anachronism. Aristotle lived some 800 years after these Trojan wars

**more deaf than adders:** adders were commonly believed to lack hearing. Refers to the Bible, Psalms 58:4–5

**partial indulgence ... resist the same:** through frequent gratification of the senses the will is corrupted

**no mean dependence ... several dignities:** our individual and collective honour is greatly affected

**canonise us:** make us famous and renowned

---

**Act II Scene 3:** *the Greek camp before Achilles's tent*

---

The previous scene, which depicted the Trojans nobly discussing the problems of value and the motives for action, is quickly undercut by a scene which centres on intrigue, false flattery and vicious backbiting.

In soliloquy, Thersites invokes vengeance, more particularly the boneache or syphilis that descends on the whole camp as a fitting punishment for those who war for a woman of loose morals such as Helen.

As 'privileged' railer, Thersites sets out to prove that the Greek camp is run by fools. He sees through the knavery of playing one faction against another. He comments bitterly, reducing the principle of war to its lowest denominators: 'all the argument is a cuckold and a whore'.

After repeated rebuffs by Achilles, Agamemnon himself arrives to assert his identity, rank and place as central ruler. He urges Patroclus and Ulysses to inform Achilles (sulking in his tent again) that unless he can use his prowess to help the Greek war effort they will refuse to deal with him any longer.

Ulysses reports that Achilles's 'imagined worth' makes him follow his individual bent against the needs of the community: 'Kingdom'd Achilles in commotion rages and batters down himself'. When this deputation proves a failure, Ajax undergoes the 'dressing up in voices' as the alternative Greek hero.

NOTES AND GLOSSARY

**carry it:** come out on top, lord it over

**'s foot:** an oath,—'by God's foot'.

**O thou great thunder-darter ... little wit from them:** if Jove's power and Mercury's cunning do not deprive them of the little intelligence they possess, their claim to being gods is null

**serpentine craft of thy caduceus:** Mercury's wand, twined with serpents, as a symbol of his cunning

**Neapolitan bone-ache:** syphilis, a dread disease which, starting from Naples, spread to France and all over Europe in the wake of the armies

**placket:** slit or opening in skirt or petticoat. Here it stands for prostitute

**remembered a gilt counterfeit ... slipped:** wordplay on *slip* a) escape the memory b) a false copper coin plated with silver

**blood:** passions

**lazars:** lepers

**my cheese, my digestion:** Achilles argues that Thersites's foolery helps his digestion

**decline the whole question:** pun (*a*) in the grammatical sense (*b*) refuse to give a reason why Patroclus is a fool

**patchery:** trickery

**all the argument:** the whole issue of the war

**emulous factions:** rival groups

**dry serpigo:** skin eruption

**Me shent:** scolded, rebuffed or rebuked

**appertainments:** rights, prerogative relating to rank

**inveigled:** seduced, allured, attracted by fraud

**fraction:** division, split or break

**strong composure a fool could disunite:** theirs was not a strong friendship if a fool could separate them

**not for flexure:** referring to the erroneous belief that the elephant could not bend its knees

**not virtuously on his own part beheld:** not accompanied by modesty

**than in the note of judgement:** than wise men know him to be

**tend the savage strangeness he puts on:** wait upon the rude behaviour he assumes

**underwrite ... his humourous predominance:** observe the capricious whims caused by excess of humours

**pettish lunes:** capricious, ill-humoured fits

**In will peculiar and in self-admission:** strongly approving his own obstinacy, smug and self-willed

**pride that quarrels at self-breath:** so vainglorious that he quarrels with speech itself

**Kingdom'd Achilles in commotion rages:** Achilles is compared to a kingdom engaged in civil war. Compare Brutus in Shakespeare's *Julius Caesar*, II.1.67–9

**death tokens:** symptoms, plague-spots

**bastes his arrogance . . . seam:** adds to his pride with his own fat

**stale his palm:** lessen his glory

**Cancer when he burns . . . Hyperion:** the sun, Hyperion, enters the sign of Cancer in mid-summer. If Ajax tries to convince Achilles, he will become even more proud

**he rubs the vein:** he's manipulating Ajax

**pheeze:** beat out

**let his humours blood:** cure his strangeness by blood-letting

**emulous:** a jealous rival

**thy parts of nature:** your natural gifts are three times as famous as those of other wise men

**Bull-bearing Milo:** a celebrated Greek athlete of the late sixth century who won the wrestling match six times at the Olympic games and on one occasion was said to have carried a heifer to the stadium, killed it and eaten it in one day

**a bourn, a pale:** a boundary, a fence

**the hart Achilles keeps thicket:** Achilles is spoken of as a deer afraid to venture into the open

**state of war:** council of war

**main of power:** most powerful force

---

## Act III Scene 1: *Troy—Priam's palace*

---

Pandarus excuses the absence of Troilus and prepares for the lovers' meeting in the following scene.

The scene provides the only encounter with Helen, over whom the war has raged for seven years. The atmosphere created through character, suggestive words and song is that of a genteel brothel. Paris's servant extols Helen to a transcendental goddess. This is immediately undercut by Pandarus who pretends he is talking about Cressida's 'attributes'. The audience expect another character, whose claims to real power are not genuine and cannot be supported.

Helen's entry confirms this, and Pandarus's language exposes her silliness. Rather than someone who can fire several generations with devotion, Helen is an obvious dumb beauty. The audience watch the merciless debunking of the archetypal lady of romance who sinks from 'love's invisible soul' to 'my Nell', a decadent obsessed with thoughts of love. The song with its enactment of seduction fits in with Pandarus's aim of encouraging physical love. It echoes Helen's ecstasies, anticipates the mating of Troilus and Cressida and helps set the seal on decadence.

Towards the end we have Paris's request that Helen's 'white enchanting fingers' try to 'disarm great Hector'—that Helen plays the role of 'fair lady'. Hector, who considers Helen is 'not worth the keeping' (II.1), has challenged the Greeks in the name of his own fair lady, the virtuous Andromache. Is Paris's request then a subtle attack on Hector's integrity?

NOTES AND GLOSSARY

**know me better:** here possibly Pandarus tips the servant

**in the state of grace ... my titles:** the servant hopes that Pandarus will be saved, whereas Pandarus takes *grace* to mean the courtly title of a duke, which he is not

**music in parts:** for different instruments, in counterpoint

**love's invisible soul:** the essence of spiritual love

**complimental assault:** polite exchange of praises

**my business seethes ... a stewed phrase:** word-play referring to the fact that his business (*a*) boils, is very urgent (*b*) is fit for a stews, or brothel

**broken music:** as in **music in parts** above

**bob:** cheat or defraud

**My cousin will fall out with you:** Cressida will quarrel with you

**my disposer:** the lady who governs his actions. Possibly his one-time mistress

**my niece ... a thing you have:** Cressida would like to take a lover

**they two are twain:** they have parted

**Falling in ... may make them three:** making up after a lover's quarrel may make the girl pregnant

**Shoots buck and doe:** possibly refers to Achilles. In the previous scene Ulysses refers to the 'hart [male deer] Achilles', whose love for Polyxena makes him 'keep thicket'

**confounds not that it wounds:** does not distress what it hurts

**they die:** they make love

**doth turn oh! oh! to ha! ha! he!:** changes pain to pleasure

**he eats nothing but doves:** doves and quails were said to be an aphrodisiac

**love a generation of vipers:** refers to the Bible, Matthew: 3:7; 12:34
**To a hair:**      refers to the joke about the hair which so annoyed
                 Paris in I.2.166–8
**unarm our Hector:** help Hector take off his armour
**palm:**          glory

---

## Act III Scene 2: *Pandarus's orchard*

---

As he waits in expectation of the love tryst, Troilus is typical of the pale distracted courtly lover. He takes on a fantastic romantic pose that is only gently punctured by Pandarus's realistic reply: 'Walk here in th' orchard, I'll bring her straight.'

Pandarus's main concern here, as pandar, witness and 'priest', is to lead the symbolic ceremonies of betrothal and marriage towards consummation. Initially, Cressida is a fearful loving innocent. Her 'fears have eyes', she has a premonition their love will end in suffering, and Pandarus has to keep pushing the lovers into each others' arms.

Despite her later claims to a pretence that shows 'more craft than love', Cressida's protestations of love seem sincere. She is, however, unsure of her bearings:

> I have a kind of self resides with you,
> But an unkind self that itself will leave
> To be another's fool.

This anticipates a divided personality that suggests inconstancy, but at this stage she does not swear falsely to Troilus.

The oath-swearing contest is presented emblematically. The balanced repetitions—'as true as . . .' by Troilus, 'as false as . . .' by Cressida—stress the irony of the situation, and anticipate Cressida's betrayal.

Pandarus is obviously pleased with a task accomplished, and would cheerfully act as go-between for 'all tongue-tied maidens' in the audience. This satisfaction should be contrasted with his bitter address at the end of the play (V.10.46–55).

NOTES AND GLOSSARY
**Stygian banks staying for waftage:** waiting to cross the Styx, main river
                 of the underworld
**Charon:**       the boatman in Greek mythology who ferried
                 departed souls to Hades, the underworld
**fly with me to Cressid:** Troilus is but a few metres away
**watery palate:**   similar to mouth watering at sight of tasty morsel

**thrice repured:** finely distilled, purified

**frayed with a sprite:** frightened or startled by a ghost

**my powers their bestowing lose:** I lose my composure, my calm

**like vassalage ... the eye of majesty:** like a dependent or bondman on meeting the sovereign. Compare the Sun's and king's 'medicinable eye' (I.3.91)

**watched ere you be made tame:** hawks were tamed by being continuously kept awake, watched

**put you i' th' fills:** control animal's freedom by putting it in the shafts of a cart

**draw this curtain:** Cressida was wearing a veil

**rub on, kiss the mistress:** move closer and touch. Here using the register of a game of bowling, which is known as 'rubber'. The small bowl, or 'mistress' controlled the position of the others

**a kiss in fee-farm:** never-ending kiss. A grant of land in fee was one in perpetuity, forever

**the falcon as the tercel:** the female hawk is just as willing as the male

**'In witness whereof the parties interchangeably':** the legal form for the contract of betrothal

**The gods grant ... sudden abruption:** here Cressida breaks off in fear. Compare also Troilus's reaction (IV.4.24–9 'the blest gods, as angry ... take thee from me')

**too curious dreg:** do not blemish our love by looking at it too closely

**Nothing but our undertakings:** with reference to the code of chivalry where the knight undertook virtually impossible tasks to prove his devotion

**the voice of lions and the act of hares:** those who boast much more than they perform

**no perfection in reversion ... humble:** we shall not exaggerate our claims

**what envy ... mock for his truth:** the worst that malice can do is mock Troilus's loyalty

**your silence, ... soul of counsel:** Cressida means that Troilus remained silent to discover her innermost thoughts

**I have a kind of self ... another's fool:** Cressida is drawn both ways—her policy of masking her real feelings (I.2.295–6) and her passionate desires

**keep her constancy in plight and youth:** remain as loyal as when she first promised

**beauties outward:** external beauty

**winnowed purity:** strained or sifted, free of impurities

**tired with iteration:** bored with repeating the same similes

**plantage to the moon:** vegetation was supposed to be controlled by the moon's influence

**turtle to her mate:** the turtle-dove was a symbol of fidelity

**iron to adamant:** as iron is drawn by the magnet or lodestone

**mighty states characterless are grated:** all records of great city states are destroyed

**Pard to the hind:** leopard to the female deer

**let all constant men be Troiluses:** the grammatical sense requires *inconstant*, but Pandarus's slip might have been occasioned by the previous repetition of 'true' for Troilus

---

**Act III Scene 3:** *the Greek camp*

---

This second longest scene falls into three divisions: Calchas's request, the education of Achilles, and the pageant of Ajax.

Calchas convinces Agamemnon that he should negotiate the exchange of the Trojan prisoner Antenor for his daughter Cressida. Thus no sooner have Troilus and Cressida consummated their love than the process of separation begins. The atmosphere of doom expressed by Cassandra (II.2.109–12), and picked by Cressida (III.2.185–6) is now directly stated by Calchas who 'through the sight of things to come' had abandoned Troy. Diomed has the task of pressing for Cressida's release.

According to Ulysses's plan, Greek lords scornfully pass by Achilles's tent. This sets Achilles deliberating as to whether greatness is the prize of individual merit or of rank, riches and friends—accidents easily lost through change of fortune.

Ulysses's book and his studied 'derision medicinable' confirm that greatness is relative and variable. Ulysses mentions the sudden growth in Ajax's popularity. He points out to Achilles that only vigorous action in the Greek war effort can help preserve the glories, of which many rivals and calumniating time have grown envious. Ulysses surprises Achilles when he tells him that his love for Polyxena and his dealings with the Trojans are an open secret.

Achilles is now convinced that his reputation is in danger. He also feels that his destiny is strongly linked to that of the Trojan champion:

I have a woman's longing . . .
To see great Hector in his weeds of peace.

When Thersites engages with Patroclus in the 'pageant' it is more than just a parody of Ajax—indirectly it hits at Achilles's 'valiant ignorance'.

Jolted out of self-sufficiency, Achilles feels apprehensive: 'My mind is troubled like a fountain stirred'.

The image of the muddied fountain had already been used by the lovers and there it hints at the corruption of motive, and treachery.

NOTES AND GLOSSARY

**sight I bear in things to come:** my ability to read the future

**sequestering:** isolating, separating, cutting away

**in way of taste:** as a foretaste of future favours already promised

**such a wrest in their affairs:** so important in the harmonious efficient running of their policies. A **wrest** is the tuning key

**in most accepted pain:** pain willingly suffered

**unplausive eyes are bent on him:** scornful looks directed at him

**derision medicinable:** scorn that will correct Achilles's pride, just as the sun-king's 'medicinable eye' in I.3.91 corrects the evil influence of wandering stars

**supple knees ... proud man's fees:** pride feeds on and exacts adulation and praise

**show not their mealy wings but to the summer:** men act friendly when it suits them to

**a strange fellow here:** probably the Athenian philosopher Plato (429–347BC) in one of his works, *Alcibiades* I

**how dearly ever parted:** however richly gifted

**at the author's drift:** at the writer's conclusions

**where they're extended:** where his gifts are magnified

**the unknown Ajax:** who does not know himself, lacking self-knowledge

**Most abject in regard and dear in use:** mean and despicable yet very useful

**pride is fasting in his wantonness:** Achilles is capriciously abstaining in self-satisfaction

**like a rusty mail in monumental mockery:** it was the custom to hang the armour of dead knights in church

**direct forthright:** course of action indicated

**the abject rear:** the meaner soldiers who follow

**One touch of nature ... newborn gawds:** all men have one weakness in common, they love toys and novelties

**more laud then gilt o'erdusted:** more praise than gold covered with dust

**The cry went once on thee:** you were once popular

**emulous missions ... Mars to faction:** the gods made partisan warfare and even Mars, supposed to be impartial, took sides

**every grain of Pluto's gold:** the god of wealth was Plutus, while Pluto was the god of the underworld

**finds bottom in th' uncomprehensive deeps:** solves the most difficult problems

**Keeps place with thought . . . dumb cradles:** runs parallel with thought and anticipates ideas before they are expressed

**with whom relation durst never meddle:** which has not yet been accounted for

**Pyrrhus:** Achilles's son, also called Neoptolemus

**The fool slides o'er the ice that you should break:** apparently referring to *Foole upon Foole* (1600) by Robert Armin (1565?–1610) which told of an idiot who walked safely across the thinnest of ice that 'would not indure the fall of a brickbat'

**My fame is shrewdly gored:** my reputation is in danger

**Seals a commission to a blank of danger:** gives danger a free hand

**a woman's longing:** irresistible desire, the craving of a pregnant woman

**in his weeds of peace:** unarmed

**Ajax . . . asking for himself:** word-play 'Ajax' on 'a jakes' which is a lavatory

**with a politic regard:** pretending to be a wise politician

**opinion . . . like a leather jerkin:** opinions are easily contradicted

**put on his presence:** imitate him

**fiddler Apollo . . . to make catlings on:** Apollo, the god of music, makes catgut or strings for musical instruments

---

### Act IV Scene 1: *a street in Troy*

---

Events gather pace. Diomed has arrived in Troy and demanded the surrender of Cressida for the 'enfreed Antenor'. Aeneas hurries to Pandarus's house to inform Troilus of the deal.

Paris then puts the question previously discussed during the Trojan council (II.2): Who merits Helen, her husband or her lover? Diomed argues that the claims of 'cuckold and lecher' are finely balanced, but that anyway Greeks and Trojans are fighting over an unworthy cause. Helen is just a whore, over whose 'contaminated carrion weight' many have been slain. Diomed's bitterness, following the earlier pleasant gallantries, is just as devastating as Thersites's scorn.

NOTES AND GLOSSARY

**witness the process of your speech:** as you have often said

**a whole week by days:** every day for a week

**all question of the gentle truce:** while the truce lasts

**policy:** cunning and craft

**by Anchises' life ... By Venus' hand:** Aeneas first swears by his father, and then by his mother, whose hand was slightly wounded by Diomed aided by Minerva

**We sympathise:** our feelings are mutual

**constantly do think ... certain knowledge:** Paris is sure Troilus is sleeping with Cressida

**whole quality wherefore:** the reason why we come

**soilure:** dishonour

**world of charge:** great risk and cost

**not palating:** not tasting or noticing

**flat tamèd piece:** wine that has gone flat, or a woman so lascivious that she can no longer excite

**Both merits poised ... heavier for a whore:** one is as bad as the other, but because Menelaus legally possesses Helen he may be slightly heavier

**scruple ... contaminated carrion weight:** every twenty grains of Helen's dishonoured body

**chapmen:** dealer or hawker in cheap goods

---

**Act IV Scene 2:** *the court of Pandarus's house*

---

At dawn, Troilus is taking his leave of Cressida. Pandarus naughtily but gently mocks their loss of sleep.

Aeneas arrives to inform Troilus that 'the general state of Troy' had decreed that Cressida must go. Presumably Antenor is too valuable a military adviser, and love must surrender to the demands of war. Troilus does not dispute or question the decision, but he is stunned.

Pandarus, obviously concerned about Troilus, drops the saucy wit of the man of the world and speaks with feeling:

'Thou must be gone, wench, thou must be gone; thou art changed for Antenor; thou must to thy father, and be gone from Troilus: 'twill be his death, 'twill be his bane; he cannot bear it.'

The repetition of verbal structures lends his speech the air of a lament. Although her speech is full of unconscious irony, Cressida's emotions seem just as genuine: she is distressed.

NOTES AND GLOSSARY

**sleep kill those pretty eyes ... thy senses:** sleep overpower your eyes and relax your other senses. Possibly **kill** is a misreading for *lull*

**Beshrew the witch ... As tediously as hell:** curse the night, she helps evil doers

**still held off ... would have tarried:** if I had kept you off, you would
        have stayed longer
**How go maidenheads?:** are you still a virgin?
**You bring me to do ... flout me too:** you first urge me to go to bed with
        Troilus, and then you chide me
**capocchia:**      (Italian) fool or simpleton. Literally *head of a pin*
**bugbear:**      elf, fairy or goblin
**it doth import:**  it is necessary
**do not you know of him:** pretend you don't know where he is
**My matter is so rash:** my errand is urgent, pressing
**general state:**     council of elders and noblemen
**the secrets of neighbour Pandar ... taciturnity:** I shall not utter a word
**'twill be his bane:**  it will cause his destruction
**no touch of consanguinity:** no blood relation

---

### Act IV Scene 3: *a street before Pandarus's house*

A brisk scene highlighting the indecent haste with which the Trojans,
ignoring Cressida's rights as an individual, seek to clinch the bargain.
As in IV.4.143, Paris is particularly callous.

Troilus, who had led the defence of Helen in the Trojan council, is
here a passive and ineffectual 'priest'. On the altar of political expediency, he is prepared to sacrifice himself and Cressida

NOTES AND GLOSSARY
**great morning:**    broad day
**thy brother Troilus a priest:** Compare Troilus's scorn for his 'brother
        priest' Helenus in II.2.36–50

---

### Act IV Scene 4: *Pandarus's house*

Although it opens with Cressida declaiming her grief, this scene more
closely examines the shock to Troilus's sensibility.

Flanked by Cressida's slightly jarring series of questions and excla-
mations, and by Pandarus's odd moans and actions ('Let me embrace
too'), Troilus is at the centre, deeply conscious of the process of
separation.

Mocked by circumstance, Troilus feels 'injurious Time' tearing him
away from his love. The words he employs—*justles roughly, rudely
beguiles, forcibly prevents,*—stress conflict, separation and violence.
He has now shaken off the role of priest and is determined even to
corrupt the Greek sentries to visit Cressida.

However, his repeated injunctions 'be thou true' not only vex Cressida, but also betray the doubt which assails him.

This is exemplified when the Greek envoy arrives. The gallantries flare into anger when Troilus seeks to issue instructions to Diomed. Resenting Troilus, but highly praising Cressida's beauty, the quarrelsome Diomed utters his own sharp ambiguous warning: 'When I am hence, I'll answer to my lust.'

Diomed's strong will and realism are at the root of the bitter rivalry that develops.

NOTES AND GLOSSARY

**temporise ... my grief:** if I could check or humour my love, I would control my sadness

**qualifying dross:** impurity

**spectacles:** Word-play (*a*) what a sight! and (*b*) aids to sight

**injury of chance:** injurious Fortune

**beguiles our lips of all rejoindure:** prevents us kissing

**must poorly sell ourselves:** must deprive our love of the attention it deserves

**As many farewells ... loose adieu:** farewell promises and the kisses which confirm them are hurriedly pressed into one goodbye kiss

**scants us:** cheats us

**the Genius so cries 'Come!':** the guardian spirit who is mentioned in Plato's *Republic* (X, 620E). Here Plato set out a complete system for an ideal society in which guardians, or 'philosopher kings', rule in the interest of the majority who have only a limited perception

**merry Greeks:** gay irresponsible Greeks

**wicked deem:** ugly thought

**use expostulation kindly:** do not waste this opportunity in quarrelling

**throw my glove:** challenge

**maculation:** stain

**to fashion in my sequent protestation:** so that my own promise to visit you will follow

**wear this sleeve:** sleeves were detachable and often given as love tokens

**their loving ... arts and exercise:** they are well versed in the theory and practice of love

**parts with person:** skill and personal charm

**heel the high lavolt:** perform their lively dance

**prompt and pregnant:** ready and able

**dumb discoursive:** silently persuasive and eloquent

**presuming on their changeful potency:** taking for granted power that is changeable and unstable

**possess thee:** inform you

**To shame the zeal of my petition:** to scorn my earnest request

**even for my charge:** because I instruct you to do so

**privileged by my place and message:** as Greek envoy and messenger Diomed was protected

**I'll answer to my lust:** I'll do as I wish; but there may be an anticipatory warning with regard to Cressida's virtue

**brave:** boast or bravado

---

## Act IV Scene 5: *the Greek camp*

---

With lists set out, Ajax and the Greek lords wait for the arrival of Hector. But Diomed and Cressida arrive first and the Greek kissing welcome shows up the flirtatious nature of Cressida. She is forward, unabashed and at ease among the merry Greeks—skilfully taking advantage of the occasion to establish her wit. Ulysses's judgement sinks her as a 'daughter of the game'. His portrait of Troilus as 'more vindicative than jealous love' is just as accurate.

After the bloodless encounter with Ajax, Hector is praised for his chivalry and generosity: 'Jupiter ... dealing life.' Achilles, who has been oppressing Hector with his gaze, suddenly breaks out in prophetic insolence: 'Tell me ye heavens, in which part of his body shall I destroy him?'. Hector is vexed, but he goes in to feast with the Greeks.

Meanwhile, Troilus asks Ulysses to accompany him to Calchas's tent—Cressida's test is at hand.

NOTES AND GLOSSARY

**appointment:** arms, military equipment

**sphered bias cheek:** round puffed cheek

**outswell the colic of puffed Aquilon:** the North Wind, swollen as if by colic. *Colic* may be an error for *choler* (anger) or *choller* (jaw)

**early days:** too early in the day

**ken the manner of his gait:** know his walk

**kindness particular ... general:** in his own personal capacity and not as representative

**that winter:** with reference to old Nestor's kiss

**thus popped Paris ... argument:** Patroclus steps between, imitating the separating of Helen from Menelaus

**make my match to live:** wager my life

**give you boot:**    odds, advantage
**you're an odd man:** single, on your own
**fillip:**    strike
**no match, your nail against his horn:** his cuckold's horn is stronger than your nail
**There's language . . . motive of her body:** like a courtesan she attracts with her bodily movement
**encounterers . . . ere it comes:** forward persons eager to flirt
**unclasp the tables of their thoughts:** speak out their thoughts
**ticklish reader:**    wanton observer
**sluttish spoils of opportunity:** corrupt harlots easily yielding
**daughters of the game:** prostitutes
**securely done . . . misprizing:** overconfident, despising
**maiden battle:**    practice match, bloodless
**being kin/Half stints their strife:** their being relatives lessens the fury
**deedless in his tongue:** not boastful
**impair:**    vulgar, unworthy, unsuitable
**subscribes/To tender objects:** grants mercy to the weak, or the fallen
**even to his inches:**    thoroughly
**gory emulation:**    bloody rivalry
**dexter . . . sinister:** right and left, with a reference to *bar sinister*: denoting bastardy
**him that thunders:** Jove, god of thunder
**Neoptolemus:**    Pyrrhus, son of Achilles. Here probably referring to Achilles himself
**Oyez:**    'hear you' a call by the public crier to secure silence and attention before a public proclamation
**expecters of our Trojan part:** Trojans who are waiting for the outcome
**all hollow bias-drawing:** insincerities, underhand dealing, and bias such as that employed in bowling
**quondam wife:**    former wife
**labouring for destiny:** killing people marked out by destiny
**despising many forfeits and subduements:** spurning those who were wounded or had already surrendered
**shraped:**    trapped, surrounded
**grandsire:**    Laomedon, king of Troy
**chronicle:**    historian
**buss:**    kiss
**prenominate in nice conjecture:** exactly foretell
**stithied:**    forged, shaped or fashioned by fire
**general state . . . odds with him:** the commanders can scarce allow you to insult him now

**pelting:** paltry, not important
**fell:** threatening, fierce, cruel
**convive:** feast, make merry
**amorous view:** loving looks
**boasting ... a mock is due:** those who boast about their love-wounds
deserve scorn

---

**Act V Scene 1:** *the Greek camp—before Achilles's tent*

---

After the chivalry of single combat, this scene uncovers the sordid abuse
that underlies chivalric acts. This scene effectively destroys the characters of Achilles and Diomed, whose insolence grows into falsity.

Achilles anticipates the same thirst for blood that he will soon show
in his scene of greatest treachery (V.8). It is significant that Achilles,
rather than Thersites, starts the scurrilous backbiting through the
disease imagery. For the first time, he is also charged with having a
homosexual relationship with Patroclus.

On reading Hecuba's letter, he re-affirms his love for Polyxena and
his oath that he will not fight against Troy. When Hector arrives at
Achilles's tent, he is warmly welcomed and feasted.

When Diomed leaves on 'important business' to meet Cressida,
Thersites's full scorn is directed at this false Greek.

NOTES AND GLOSSARY
**batch:** quantity of loaves produced at one baking. Possibly
an error for *botch*, sore or ulcer which seems to fit
in better with the imagery of disease that follows
**thou picture of what thou seemest:** you fake! hypocrite!
**Who keeps the tent now?:** Who is still with Hector in Agamemnon's
tent?
**The surgeon's box, or the patient's wound:** Thersites wittily puns on
*tent*, a dressing of lint or gauze for cleaning a wound
**masculine whore:** homosexual
**diseases of the south:** syphilis, venereal diseases. See II.3.18
**gravel i' th' back:** kidney stones
**imposthume:** pus or abscess, decay
**lime-kilns:** scaly red patches
**fee simple of the tetter:** permanent skin eruptions
**preposterous discoveries:** possibly referring to homosexuality
**sleave-silk:** downy floss silk
**sarcenet:** taffetta, soft silk
**tassel:** ornamental pendant

**taxing me and gaging:** complaining and urging
**loves quails:** loves loose women, or prostitutes. Quails, wild fowl, were considered to be aphrodisiac
**transformation of Jupiter:** Jupiter fell in love with Europa, daughter of Agenor, King of Tyre and Sidon. Taking the shape of a white bull, he looked so gentle that Europa felt quite safe with him, and climbed on his back, whereupon the bull swam towards Crete and Jupiter made Europa his mistress
**his brother, the bull:** Menelaus who was cuckolded by Paris
**lazar:** leper
**sweet draught . . . sewer:** cesspool
**the tide whereof is now:** now is the right time
**spend his mouth . . . like Brabbler the hound:** talk without reason, like a hunting-dog who barks before even scenting the game
**leave to see:** miss seeing
**incontinent varlets:** lewd, wanton rogues

---

**Act V Scene 2:** *the Greek camp—before Calchas's tent*

---

This betrayal scene should be examined against III.2. where tenderness and love, rather than treachery and lechery, prevail.

No longer the apprehensive girl who fetches her breath 'as short as a new-taken sparrow' for the idealist Troilus, here Cressida is the experienced coquette encouraging and teasing the realist Diomed. The intention now is not romantic, but satiric—a double row of observers ensures the unmasking of Cressida.

In a scene of visual originality, Cressida stands with Diomed in the balcony. While Ulysses and Troilus eavesdrop below, they are in their turn spied upon by Thersites, who alone watches the whole proceedings. His barbs fly in two directions—towards Troilus's idealism and the courting couple's lechery.

Wanton Cressida pretends to hold back but yields even Troilus's love-token. Her villainy is such that only gradually does Troilus escape intricate argument ('This is and is not Cressida') to accept her as absolutely false.

This betrayal brings about the division that throws Troilus and ordered Nature into chaos ('The bonds of heaven are slipp'd'). Now that all his faith and idealism have been destroyed, Troilus will throw himself wholeheartedly into the war.

NOTES AND GLOSSARY

**any man may sing her ... her cliff:** she will give in to any new acquaintance. **Cliff** refers to *clef*, musical key

**she's noted:** she's notorious

**secretly open:** sexually frank in private

**flow to great distraction:** become frenzied

**luxury:** lechery, one of the seven Deadly Sins

**potato-finger:** fat finger. Potatoes were accounted aphrodisiac, stimulants to lechery

**I will, la:** I promise I will

**she sharpens; well said, whetstone!:** she sharpens Diomed's desire. Possibly refers to 'Cressid's Complaint' in *Rocke or Regard* (1576) by George Whetstone (1551–87), which warned men against 'Cressid's heiress ... cunning in wanton exercises ... incitements.'

**By all Diana's waiting-women yond:** an oath. By the stars clustered around the moon. The moon, Diana, symbolised chastity

**straight starts you:** immediately makes you angry

**I shall be plagued:** cursed or annoyed. Possibly refers to the *Testament of Cresseid* (1532) by Robert Henryson (1425–1506), where Cressida is reduced to a leper and a beggar

**the error of our eye:** our flirting roving eyes

**turpitude:** baseness, perversity

**credence ... esperance:** strong belief ... hope

**doth invert th'attest:** goes against the testimony

**deceptious:** deceiving, false, delusive

**my negation:** denial

**square the general sex by Cressid's rule:** measure all women's behaviour by Cressida's

**swagger himself out on's own eyes?:** will he argue bombastically against what he has seen?

**sanctimonies:** sacred

**If there be rule in unity itself:** if it is true that Cressida cannot be a divided self. Compare line 146: 'This is, and is not, Cressid'

**orifex:** opening

**Ariachne's broken woof:** referring to Arachne's weaving contest with Athena, which so angered the goddess that Arachne was changed into a spider

**five-finger-tied:** Cressida's hand is now clasped in Diomed's

| | |
|---|---|
| **orts:** | leftovers, scraps of food |
| **casque:** | helmet |
| **constringed:** | pressed together |
| **he'll tickle it for his concupy:** | it will only serve to increase his lechery |
| **commodious drab:** | useful obliging whore |
| **burning devil:** | venereal disease |

---

### Act V Scene 3: *Troy—before Priam's palace*

---

The doom first voiced by Cassandra envelops the Trojans. Andromache dreams shapes of slaughter, Hecuba has visions, and Priam foretells impending disaster if Hector fights that day.

Hector, however, is hedged in by his code of chivalry. He stands engaged to meet many noble Greeks in battle, and his honour overrules all evil omens.

Cassandra's failure to convince Hector to unarm can be an electrifying scene. She accurately translates future events into the present so that the audience can see shapes of slaughter and hear the echoes of Greek victory or Trojan lament: 'Look how thou diest ... Hector! Hector's dead! O Hector.' This prolepsis (assumption that something is done before it is so) controls future action and makes it inevitable.

Also anticipatory is Troilus's complaint against Hector's 'vice of mercy'. While Hector insists on fair play, Troilus himself suggests 'venom'd' vengeance and ruthlessness.

Troilus's new resolution is shown when Pandarus brings a love-letter from Cressida which is summarily dismissed as 'mere words.' This incident puts Cressida in a shocking light—taking her pleasure where she finds it, but still hedging her bets.

Originally, this scene probably contained the dismissal of Pandarus which is now found in V.10. towards the end of the play.

NOTES AND GLOSSARY

**my dreams ... ominous to the day:** my dreams are related to today's events

**The gods ... in the sacrifice:** the gods do not accept perverse vows, rather they consider them unworthy

**keeps the weather:** seeks to control, and maintain advantage

**brushes of the war:** battles, scuffles

**better fits a lion than a man:** in his *Natural History* (chapter 16), the Roman author Pliny the Elder (AD23–79) notes that alone among the animals the lion spares those who humbly submit to him

**rein them from ruth:** keep them from pity
**Beckoning with fiery truncheon my retire:** referring to the practice of
signalling end of the fight by showing the staff of
office
**o'ergalled:** swollen and inflamed
**crutch ... stay:** means of support
**the faith of valour:** a brave man's word
**shame respect:** neglect my duty as a son
**bodements:** portents of disaster
**dolours:** sorrows
**witless antics:** madmen
**tisick:** consumptive cough
**errors:** lies

---

**Act V Scene 4:** *field between Troy and the Greek camp*

Thersites intensifies his attack on wars and lechery. His description of
the warriors battling for the 'sleeve' reduce them to ridicule, while his
suggestion that they are likely to have swallowed each other, 'lechery
eats itself,' connects with the statement on Appetite in I.3.120. that
gains significance as the play approaches its climax.

Thersites's reflections on Greek policy are just as reductive—despite
Ulysses's manoeuvring, Ajax and Achilles are refusing to fight. The
situation is such that confidence in a central authority is lost, and
'barbarism' proclaimed. The following seven scenes—really one long
battle scene—translate into actuality the chaos that follows the weakening of order and degree.

NOTES AND GLOSSARY
**clapper-clawing:** manhandling, mauling, mangling
**sleeveless:** useless, futile
**proclaim barbarism:** accepting the rule of chaos
**withdrew me from the odds of multitude:** I retired to avoid too great a
disadvantage

---

**Act V Scene 5:** *the battlefield*

Trojan military exploits are noted. Hector and Troilus both cover
themselves in glory, and total defeat stares the Greeks in the face. But
the death of Patroclus stings Achilles into action. Ajax too is arming,
cursing, vowing vengeance. Achilles rages: 'I will none but Hector.'

NOTES AND GLOSSARY
**chastised the amorous Trojan:** beaten Troilus
**The fierce Polydamas ... our numbers:** only William Caxton's *Recuyell of the Historyes of Troye* (*c.*1474) names all these combats and combatants
**colossus-wise:** like the huge bronze statue of the sun God Helios standing at the entrance to the harbour at Rhodes, which was one of the seven wonders of the world. It was destroyed by an earthquake in 224BC
**beam:** spear
**Sagittary:** a centaur, half man and half horse. An accurate archer who caused havoc among the Greeks
**scaléd sculls:** scaly shoals of fish
**strawy Greeks, ripe for his edge:** ready to be mown down by Hector's sword or spear
**proof is called impossibility:** even visible proof is not believed
**boy-queller:** boy-killer, referring to the slaying of Patroclus

---

**Act V Scene 6:** *another part of the field*

---

Despite his boasts, Achilles is immediately in difficulty and Hector's 'mercy' spares his life. Achilles retires, vowing revenge.

Then occurs Hector's ruthless hunting of the knight 'in sumptuous armour'. Temporarily overcome by Appetite, Hector dispenses with his usual courtesy and generosity to hunt the cowardly Greek 'for thy hide'.

This fits in well, however, with Caxton's description of Hector as a 'wolf ravysshyng and insatiable' and again connects with the 'appetite, an universal wolf' image in Ulysses's speech on Degree (I.3.120).

Hector's fall from chivalry will soon be punished by death.

NOTES AND GLOSSARY
**would correct him:** punish him
**cogging:** cheating
**reck not:** do not care
**frush:** batter, beat upon

---

**Act V Scene 7:** *another part of the field*

---

A short scene that undercuts the deeds of war. The battlefield becomes a bear-garden.

It makes fun of Menelaus and Paris, the cuckold and the cuckold-maker; further establishes the cowardice of Thersites; and above all considerably reduces the stature of the greatest Greek warrior. Unable to beat Hector in fair combat, Achilles resorts to the 'policy' he would have condemned earlier. Surrounded by his Myrmidons, he instructs them in treachery, and with the odds stacked heavily in his favour, re-starts the hunt for Hector.

NOTES AND GLOSSARY
**empale him:**     shut him in
**in fellest manner execute your arms:** kill Hector most cruelly
**Now, bull! now, dog! 'Loo:** cries to incite dogs in baiting a bear in a bear-garden
**Ware horns:**     beware of the Menelaus's horns

---

**Act V Scene 8:** *another part of the field*

---

In the war climax, Hector enters carrying the body of the knight whose 'goodly armour hath cost thy life.' The dramatic irony in Hector's words stresses the symbolic significance of this scene—appetite, momentarily rendering him defenceless. As John Lydgate (1370–1451), in *The Hystorye Sege and Destruccyon of Troye* (1513), complains:

Alas why was he [Hector] so rekles,
This floure of knyghtehood, of manhode pereless!

At this stage Achilles and his Myrmidons strike at the unarmed Hector. Achilles then adds dishonesty to treachery in claiming 'Achilles hath the mighty Hector slain,' bloodthirstiness to pride in his dese-cration of the body of his enemy.

NOTES AND GLOSSARY
**vail and darking:**   sinking and darkening
**forego this vantage:** do not take advantage
**stickler-like:**     like an umpire
**tie his body to my horse's tail:** According to Caxton's *Recuyell of the Hystoryes of Troye*, Achilles meted this abject treatment to Troilus whose body he bound 'to the tail of his horse and so drew it after him'

---

**Act V Scene 9:** *another part of the field*

---

Throughout the Greek army, Achilles's boastful lie re-echoes: 'Hector's slain, and by Achilles'. Only Ajax pays tribute to Hector's greatness—while the others are more concerned with the 'conversion' of Achilles.

There is every indication that Troy without Hector will soon collapse. Agamemnon seems to think that Hector's death will unite the Greeks once more in their respect for order and authority, away from barbarism.

NOTES AND GLOSSARY
**bruit:**            rumour, claim, report

---

**Act V Scene 10:** *another part of the field*

---

As news of Hector's death echoes the 'sure destruction' of Troy, Troilus's hate becomes more universal, centring particularly on Achilles. The Greeks, who appeared strong, skilful and valiant in the first scene, are now vile, abominable and cowardly. The Trojans are subdued, resigned to their fate, but dignified in grief: 'Hector is dead; there is no more to say.'

As the play moves uncertainly away from the finality of this 'ending', we get a promise of poetic justice in the second ending:

> Strike a free march to Troy! with comfort go:
> Hope of revenge shall hide our inward woe.

But this also turns out to be a false ending. Incongruously, the go-between Pandarus turns up on the battlefield and is scornfully 'dismissed'. There is no conclusive evidence that this dismissal and farewell oration of Pandarus were originally meant to be performed only before a rowdy student audience during an Inn of Court Revels performance.

As it now stands, the play has a dramatically neat circular structure. Disillusion and bitterness engulf not only the idealist Troilus, but even the hardened Pandarus, who shrugs off Troilus's curse by making an indecent, offensive attempt on the audience's sensibility—thus ensuring a satiric exit to a potential tragedy.

NOTES AND GLOSSARY
**starve we out:**       endure the freezing night
**smite:**            strike, hit. Quarto and Folio versions read *smile*, probably a misreading
**brief plagues be mercy:** show pity in sending plagues which quickly destroy us
**imminence:**        impending circumstance or event
**screech-owl:**       traditionally a bearer of bad news
**Niobes:**           Niobe, whose twelve children were killed by Apollo and Diana, was herself changed into a constantly weeping stone
**pight:**             pitched

**Titan:** the sun

**great-siz'd coward:** Achilles

**wicked conscience ... mouldeth goblins:** a guilty imagination that conjures ghosts or spirits

**broker-lackey:** pandar, go-between

**painted cloths:** imitation tapestry, sometimes bearing slogans or maxims

**hold-door trade:** debauchery and prostitution

**gallèd goose of Winchester:** a prostitute, probably diseased. This refers to the brothels in the Southwark district of London, under the jurisdiction of the Bishop of Winchester

**sweat:** a common treatment for venereal disease

# Part 3

# Commentary

## Theme

*Troilus and Cressida* is concerned with opposed and contradictory views. Theme, character and action are explored in unorthodox, unusual methods. These result in ambiguity which in turn enforces uneasiness. That is one reason why this fascinating play has never been popular.

Critics have argued that the root of this contradiction must be sought in historical biography. Some read Cressida as the 'dark lady' of the Sonnets, others see Achilles as a parallel to Essex, and argue that the crises experienced by Troilus reflected Shakespeare's own bewildered spirit, his growing conviction that 'chaos is the ultimate state of being'.

There is no need, however, to insinuate the 'mythical sorrows' of Shakespeare to account for disturbing elements in the play. Nor need they be traced to the pessimism prevalent at the turn of the century, classical or mediaeval literary sources, contemporary 'wars of the theatre' or dramatic convention. These are valid approaches, but must not predetermine Shakespeare's drama. On the other hand, close concentration on the dramatic text, the inter-relatedness of theme, character and action provide the basis for analysis and interpretation.

Ever since F.S. Boas coined the term 'problem play' for Shakespeare's canon, *Troilus and Cressida* has been so classified, since it consistently raises problems of classification and interpretation. Most often with *All's Well* and *Measure for Measure*, it has been described as dark, bitter, cynical, perplexing and painful. Dealing as they do with highly artificial 'rotten' societies:

> throughout these plays we move along dim untrodden paths, and at
> the close our feeling is neither of simple joy or pain ... the issues
> raised preclude a completely satisfactory outcome.*

After examining the reaction of the audience, W.W. Lawrence pointed out that, as distinct from a problem in mathematics where a single true solution is possible, this play explores problems of conduct that admit of different interpretations.† To complicate matters, in *Troilus and*

* F.S. Boas, *Shakespeare and his Predecessors*, John Murray, London, 1896, p.345

† W.W. Lawrence, *Shakespeare's Problem Comedies*, Macmillan, New York, 1931, p.4

*Cressida* problems of origin, classification and performance have often merged into problems of interpretation, and often predetermined a reading of the text.

The 1603 entry in the Stationers' Register and the original but cancelled title-page of the 1609 Quarto—'The Historie of Troylus and Cresseida as it was acted by the Kings Maiestis servants at the Globe'—suggest that the play was performed in open competition with plays such as Henry Chettle's (*d*. 1607) *troyless and creseda*. However, many have argued that *Troilus and Cressida* was written for a 'private' production for the Termers of the Inns of Court, who relished the 'deliberate flouting of tradition as established by Chaucer and Homer.'*

The 1623 Folio edition urges a different classification—a 'Tragedie' instead of 'Historie'. It is well to realise however, that both the 'fierce Prologue' and 'salacious epilogue'—without which, Coghill argues, the play emerges as a tragedy 'in line with the belief that the English were descended from the Trojans'†—appear in the Folio (which calls it a Tragedy), but are missing in the Quarto (which calls it a History).

Moreover the hard-sell approach of the 1609 Quarto epistle stresses the comic aspects that went into the writing of the play:

> A new play, never stal'd with the Stage ... yet passing full of the palme comicall; shewing such a dexteritie, and power of witte, that the most displeased with Playes, are pleased with his Commedies. Amongst all there is none more witty than this.

The story of Troy, culminating here in the death of Hector, is essentially tragic. On the other hand, the comedy and satire are not restricted to Prologue and epilogue.

Even without Prologue and unconventional ending, the play would not emerge as a 'Tragedy on the heroic and traditional theme of Troy'.‡ The body of the play testifies to satiric undercurrents. Mock-heroic elements in plot and character continually undercut the tragic and heroic tone inherent in Shakespeare's sources. The play is then a curious amalgam deriving its humour from absurd, grotesque, unpleasant and even tragic situations. Throughout, the ruthless unruffled 'temper of the Inquisitor' explores the motives of characters, controls their emotions, and prevents the sympathy of the audience.**

* Peter Alexander, 'Troilus and Cressida', *The Library*, Oxford University Press, Oxford, 1928, pp.267–86

† Nevill Coghill, *Shakespeare's Professional Skills*, Cambridge University Press, Cambridge, 1960, p.78.

‡ Nevill Coghill, Ibid.

** A.P. Rossiter, *Angel with Horns*, Longman, London, 1961, p.111.

The juxtaposition of tragedy and comedy has prompted critics to suggest that the play's effect is spasmodic and inconsistent because of the fact, 'however unpalatable', as J.M. Nosworthy said, that Shakespeare changed horses in midstream:

> Following upon *Hamlet*, he set to work upon another tragedy based on the pathetic story of Troilus and Cressida ... On the basis of the foregoing scenic analysis it is reasonable to surmise that he had written rather more than half the tragedy when he suddenly changed his plans and turned the whole thing into comedy.*

On the basis of predominance of comic and serious moods in the following scenic analysis (except for V.8. differing only slightly from Nosworthy's) the opposite seems to be true.

Prologue —promises serious action at heroic level, but contains deflationary elements.

I.1. —mainly comic, Pandarus undercutting Troilus's image as courtly lover.

I.2. —mainly comic, Pandarus and Cressida revelling in bawdy repartee.

I.3. —serious, discussions on dissension in the Greek camp.

II.1. —comic, Thersites's invective against dull-witted Ajax.

II.2. —serious, Trojan council arguing the 'merits' of Helen.

II.3. —comic, includes the 'dressing up in voices' of Ajax as new champion.

III.1. —comic, the exquisite deflation of silly fair Helen.

III.2. —serious, the love-night of Troilus and Cressida.

III.3. —mixed, Ulysses's lecture to Achilles on 'reputation', and the funny 'pageant of Ajax'.

IV.1–4 —serious throughout, leading to the separation of the lovers.

IV.5. —serious, except for Cressida's 'kissing welcome' by the Greeks, which is followed by single combat.

V.1. —mixed, Achilles welcomes Hector to his tent, Thersites's scurrility becoming more intense and virulent.

V.2. —serious, Troilus watches Cressida give in to Diomed.

V.3. —serious, Cassandra and the 'night of shapes' do not dissuade Hector from going to battle.

V.4. —mainly comic, with Thersites's description of the battling rivals.

V.5. —serious. After the slaying of Patroclus, Achilles seeks out Hector.

* J.M. Nosworthy, *Shakespeare's Occasional Plays*, Edward Arnold, London, 1965, p.74.

V.6.     —serious. Hector's 'vice of mercy' spares Achilles but hunts the knight 'in sumptuous armour'.

V.7.     —mixed. Achilles instructs his Myrmidons in treachery, cowardly Thersites is dismissed by Margarelon.

V.8.     —tragic, Achilles murders the unarmed Hector.

V.9.     —serious, news of Hector's death reaches the Greeks.

V.10.    —serious, news of Hector's death reaches the Trojans, doom of Troy implied, Troilus promises revenge and dismisses Pandarus.

epilogue —Pandarus insults the audience.

*Troilus and Cressida*, however, is a play with a message. Besides telling a story, the main lines of the plot also explore a theme. A.P. Rossiter succinctly summarised the theme as 'the disorderly house of man (amorous and military) turned into chaos by the egoisms of pride and lust.'*

In Homeric and mediaeval sources, love and war shaped an excuse for exploits of chivalry, honour and renown. In *Troilus and Cressida* these are continually examined, distorted or subverted.

Love and war are under scrutiny. Troilus finds 'goodness' in the quarrel, but Hector who examines the death-ratio argues that every slain soldier 'hath been as dear as Helen'. However, Hector sacrifices the 'way of truth' for expediency. Will has taken over from Reason:

And Appetite, an universal wolf, . . .
Must make perforce an universal prey,
And last eat up himself.

(I.3.121)

This assumes tragic significance in Hector's hunting the knight 'in sumptuous armour' for his hide. Hector's concupiscence and fall from chivalry there lead to the war-climax and constitute the major theme of the play: 'Most putrefied core, so fair without' (V.8.1.)

The contrast between appearance and reality is central in Shakespeare's problem plays. In *Troilus and Cressida* the contrast between seeming and being is pervasive. The rift between what 'Sun' figures promise and what they deliver uncovers the irony that is rooted in the play.

It is when motives unfold in action that characters are revealed. This entails at least a double approach in the assessment of character: first, direct self-explanation of character in statement and action, second, character as reflected in the minds of others.

* A.P. Rossiter, *Angel with Horns*, Longman, London, 1961, p.120

# Characterisation: love

## Troilus

Troilus, on whom so much depends, is a divided self—a contradiction between lover and warrior. His frustrated love dulls, rather than inspires, zeal for action:

> Why should I war without the walls of Troy
> That find such cruel battle within?
>
> (I.1.1.)

A wan romantic in love with 'stubborn-chaste' Cressida, he thinks he cannot win her without help from her uncle Pandarus. Hopelessly infatuated, he lists her virtues in courtly love tradition. He is a maker of images which translate his situation to fable and romance:

> Her bed is India; there she lies, a pearl ...
> Ourself the merchant, and this sailing Pandar,
> Our doubtful hope, our convoy and our bark.
>
> (I.1.102)

His neatly wrought sentences, with their fine balance and antithesis, establish his character. He is a student of rhetoric:

> The Greeks are strong, and skilful to their strength,
> Fierce to their skill, and to their fierceness valiant,
> But I am weaker than a woman's tear,
> Tamer than sleep, fonder than ignorance,
> Less valiant than the virgin in the night,
> And skilless as unpractised infancy.
>
> (I.1.7)

This strain of inferiority is sounded again when he is about to surrender Cressida (IV.4.76–8). He is obviously in doubt, fearful for Cressida, and jealous of the more accomplished Greeks.

As a lover he is physically innocent, but his sensual imagery has prompted O.J. Campbell to define him as a practised sensualist whom Shakespeare meant to reject.* However, Troilus is not viciously addicted. Sensuality is present but it is rooted in his youthful expectation of 'imaginary relish':

---

* O.J. Campbell, *Comicall Satyre and Shakespeare's Troilus and Cressida*, Huntingdon Library Publications, San Marino, 1938, p.212

And give me swift transportance to those fields
Where I may wallow in the lily beds ...

I am giddy: expectation whirls me round.
Th' imaginary relish is so sweet
That it enchants my sense.

(III.2.11;18)

He is not concerned merely with body. There is a strong element of the spiritual in his love:

To feed for aye her lamp and flame of love ...
Outliving beauties outward, with a mind
That doth renew swifter than blood decays!

(III.2.159)

This makes him more of the ideal romantic than a sexual gourmet. Troilus does not immediately 'walk in' when invited by Cressida; and, despite the pandar's presence, he brings out the best in her. For him Cressida represents a religion, and he is a priest to that religion:

Think it an altar, and thy brother Troilus
A priest, there offering to it his own heart.

(IV.3.7)

It is this spiritual element that so tortures his mind when his goddess turns false. The 'bonds of heaven are slipped' when he sees a lust-ridden Cressida give in to Diomed. This twists his love into a career of hatred on the battlefield to confirm Ulysses's description of him as 'more vindicative than jealous love' (IV.5.107). The mental shock of Cressida's treachery cures him of his infatuation.

As a debater, Troilus engages in the defence of Helen. He knows there are 'fools on both sides', but votes for continuing the war because she possesses symbolic value. 'A theme of honour and renown' (II.2.199). This romantic ideal represents his egoism in disguise, for he is extremely conscious of his role. As a symbol for constancy future lovers will 'approve their truths by Troilus' (III.2.173), while his prowess in war may erect him into a symbol for valour: 'And fame in time to canonise us.' (II.2.202). He is fond of argument, but this is emotional. He is therefore scornful and dismissive of the 'crammed reason' of those who support Helen's surrender:

'Reason and respect make livers pale and lustihood deject.' (II.2.51). Despite this he still seeks to protect his public image after the Trojan council's decision to exchange Cressida for Antenor. He does not protest, he knows the rules of war:

> I will go meet them; and, my Lord Aeneas,
> We met by chance: you did not find me here.
>
> (IV.2.70)

As a warrior he is intitially weakened by love, but does not give himself
to dissipation as Paris and Achilles do. Aware of his public duties,
Troilus realises 'womanish it is to be from hence' and joins Aeneas on
the battle-field. His valour is never in doubt. In the final battle he
emerges as a truly great warrior, saving Aeneas, fighting Diomed and
Ajax, doing 'mad and fantastic execution' (V.5.38).

After Hector's murder, he assumes the Trojan leadership, but he
becomes fatalistic and prays the gods to hasten 'our sure destructions
on'. Despite Aeneas's advice not to demoralise the army, he can only
offer anger and revenge. Disillusion in love and war have matured him
but he has no other option:

> Strike a free march to Troy! with comfort go:
> Hope of revenge shall hide our inward woe.
>
> (V.10.30)

## Cressida

As Troilus is fond of rhetoric, Cressida is fond of her own wit. She is
a coquette revelling in repartee and clever bawdy. In her first scene
(I.2), Cressida speaks sixty-eight times, ably controlling and directing
Alexander's and Pandarus's longer speeches. Most of her interventions
are single-line witty comments that help distance her from the audience.
Her indecent puns un-idealise the goddess of Troilus's imagination. In
plain prose she explains at what 'ward' she lies:

> Upon my back, to defend my belly; upon my wit, to defend my
> wiles ... I can watch you for telling how I took the blow; unless it
> swell past hiding, and then it's past watching.
>
> (I.2.261)

She knows the terrain and when she switches to verse she even offers
some advice:

> Therefore this maxim out of love I teach:
> 'Achievement is command; ungained, beseech.'
>
> (I.2.293)

She is not, however, a 'connoisseur of lust'. Not even a widow as she
is in Chaucer, she desires a lover, but she is still a beginner, unpractised,

and fearful. Pandarus's description of her as 'she fetches her breath as short as a new taken sparrow' (III.2.34) suggests she is still a virgin. Troilus has had to lay siege for several months.

Cressida initially believes she will be faithful. Only later does she complacently assume that hers is normal female behaviour, 'the error of our eye directs our mind' (V.2.110). But having lost her virginity, the 'eye of majesty', with which Troilus invests her, becomes suspect. Led into temptation she turns out to be very fickle, and now much more permissive for then 'it's past watching' (I.2.270). Earlier, however, she was a woman divided:

> I have a kind of self resides with you,
> But an unkind self that itself will leave
> To be another's fool.
>
> (III.2.147)

This poses problems of interpretation. Neville Coghill calls Cressida a 'chameleon', reacting and changing colour with her surroundings.* She is seen through several phases—bawdy with Pandarus, earnest with Troilus, by herself calculating, merry with the generals, and lecherous with Diomed. In parting from Troilus she shows genuine emotion, but Troilus knows she is essentially weak:

> And sometimes we are devils to ourselves,
> When we will tempt the frailty of our powers,
>
> (IV.4.95)

Having crossed over to the Greek lines her complexity vanishes. She becomes an opportunist and lecher, the Cressida of tradition, a simile for deceit. On the next night after her 'marriage' to Troilus, she takes on a new lover.

Although she pretends to waver, she is shown in descent, her delaying tactics a 'whetstone' to sharpen Diomed's desire. She even surrenders her 'sleeve' to Troilus's rival. Her worst aspect is seen when she confirms Thersites's assessment of her as a seemer and dissembler (V.4.7.). By sending the letter to Troilus she has moved from weakness and lechery to falseness. Cunning and secretive, she tries to keep Troilus hoping—just in case. She is determined to be a survivor. Troilus, however, sees through her deceit:

> My love with words and errors still she feeds,
> But edifies another with her deeds.
>
> (V.3.111)

---

* Nevil Coghill, *Shakespeare's Professional Skills*, p.107

## Diomed

The last character in this love triangle is Diomed, trusted envoy and hardy Greek warrior. Ruthless, cautious, and unforgiving, he shows little of the 'aspiration that lifts him from the earth' with which Ulysses credits him.

There is a touch of chivalry in his character when Paris is reporting Diomed's hunting out of Aeneas 'a whole week by days'. His haughtiness, directness and realism spell out the danger to Cressida's loyalty. In his assessment of Helen and the war, Diomed is most bitter. Helen is 'contaminated carrion weight' (IV.1.73). He strongly condemns Helen not on moral grounds but for the loss of 'wealth and friends'. He is libertine, faithless and a dissembler. There is a threat lurking beneath his ambiguity: 'When I am hence, I'll answer to my lust.' (IV.1.71) With the possible exception of Menelaus, Thersites scorns no one more than Diomed, whom he always associates with lust:

How the devil luxury, with his fat rump and potato-finger, tickles these together! Fry, lechery, fry

(V.2.56)

What we see of Diomed as lover confirms this. He is the typical prize-fighter, a bruiser, and flesh is what he's after. In the 'seduction' scene no warmth or love is generated, only determination and lust. Cressida knows he has no real feeling for her: 'Twas one that loved me better than you will.' (V.2.90)

That is why Diomed takes pleasure in ignoring Troilus during the prisoner's exchange (IV.4.116), in grieving 'his spirit that dares not challenge' the sleeve, and in sending Troilus's captured horse to Cressida to show he is 'her knight by proof' (V.5.5.). Increasingly, towards the end, he becomes a target for Thersites's satire whose burlesque equates him to the thing he sought for—a sleeve.

## Helen and Paris

The five main strands of *Troilus and Cressida*—love, war, policy, doom and deflation—are bound together in the origin of the Trojan War, the rape of the fair Helen by Paris. After seven years of war, Nestor makes a peace-move: Deliver Helen and all else will be forgotten. The question the Trojan council debates is not 'Was Helen worth seven years of war?' but 'Is Helen worth continuing the war?'

The Greeks think she is not, but her surrender will save their honour.

The Trojan Hector at first answers the question directly: 'She is not worth what she doth cost the holding.' (II.2.51). But Helen possesses the idea of the beautiful. She has become a symbol, a pearl 'whose price hath launched above a thousand ships' (II.2.82), inspiring generations of princes and soldiers:

> Well may we fight for her whom we know well
> The world's large spaces cannot parallel.
>
> (II.2.161)

For Troilus too she is a 'theme of honour and renown' (II.2.199), but when she comes on the stage she reveals herself as affected—the 'infinite variety' of a Cleopatra is never seen. Before she enters, however, there is an ironic build-up, 'the heart blood of beauty, love's indivisible soul.' This is immediately followed by a merciless tearing-down that is accomplished not only by Pandarus's repetitive epithets of *fair* and *sweet* as by her own satiric presentation: 'Let thy song be love; this love will undo us all. O Cupid, Cupid, Cupid!' (III.1.110)

Pandarus's bawdy song acts out her continued dissipation. She is an agent of lethargy, and Paris's request to her to help 'disarm' Hector with her 'white enchanting fingers' suggests she is a corrupting influence as well (III.1.151–55). This request is presumably an attempt to use love to manipulate policy, to draw Hector firmly onto the side of those who want to continue the war. Paris is never shown in a favourable light. A first report of Paris being 'gored with Menelaus's horn' turns out to be false, but it stresses his role as cuckold-maker.

An experienced debater, he glorifies Helen as an idea for whom generous spirits have 'a heart to dare a sword to draw'. He reminds the Council of its previous unanimous consent in the rape of Helen, invokes Trojan honour, and argues they ought not to yield 'on terms of base compulsion'.

Priam accuses him of being 'besotted'. He has been lulled into military inaction: 'I would fain have armed today but my Nell would not have it so.' (III.1.136)

When it comes to the surrender of Cressida, he blames 'the bitter disposition of the times', and is insincere and unfeeling when he claims the single combat will be late starting because Troilus has spent too long taking his farewell of Cressida: 'Tis Troilus's fault'. (IV.4.144)

The last time we see him in direct action he is being made fun of as he engages in battle with Menelaus: 'Ware horns, ho!' (V.7.12)

# Policy

## Priam

Among the Trojans, there is no strong tradition for policy. It has been suggested they stand for emotion and intuition whereas the Greeks stand for reason.

The aged Priam is a respected figure-head but he is inefficient and insignificant. He is the god-sun-king of Troy, but Nestor's peace moves are relayed to Hector who must take the initiative. Priam intervenes only twice throughout the play, first to check 'besotted' Paris, and second to prevent Hector going to battle on the day of 'shapes of slaughter'. On each occasion, he is argued out of his position.

Antenor, who is 'such a wrest in their affairs' (III.3.23), could have been the only real strategist and policy-maker but he is, surprisingly, absent from the Trojan debate. As it is, however, he is early taken prisoner, forwards the love-plot by the Cressida exchange, but does not utter one word. The real decisions are taken by Hector and Troilus.

Ironically, Hecuba and Polyxena (who are not among the *dramatis personae*) are the counterparts to Ulysses and Nestor. They foil the carefully prepared plan for getting Achilles into battle-gear (V.138–43).

## Agamemnon

Agamemnon was, by status and tradition, the great sun-king-god figure,

> ... whose medicinable eye
> Corrects the influence of evil planets,
> And posts, like the commandment of a king,
> Sans check to good and bad.

> (I.3.89)

But he is as inefficient as Priam, and not so respected. He is linked to Stoic fortitude but not to Stoic wisdom. Accepting the 'protractive trials' of Jove, he is unaware of the reasons for the Greek failure to take Troy. Ulysses uncovers the root causes as emulation and dissension. 'Troy in our weakness stands', argues Ulysses, and that weakness is embodied in Agamemnon who fails to unite the Greeks:

> When that the general is not like the hive
> To whom the foragers shall all repair,
> What honey is expected?

> (I.3.81)

Ajax and Achilles go their own way. Thersites asserts Agamemnon has no real policy, 'no matter comes from him' (II.1.5). Achilles and Patroclus act out his 'greatness ... like a chime a-mending' (I.3.159). This insignificance is stressed when Aeneas, delivering Hector's challenge, fails to recognise this 'god in office, guiding men.' (I.3.231). There is unconscious irony in Agamemnon's assurance:

> That thou shalt know, Trojan, he is awake
> He tells thee so himself.
>
> (I.3.255)

Despite Agamemnon's insistence on rank, 'the question of our place' (II.3.81), the language and methods he uses undercut his authority. Weak, he is completely guided by Ulysses, allows himself to be drawn in the fake lottery, returns the strategist Antenor to Troy, and is a constant target for Thersites's satire. Thersites relates the diseases of the camp to his inability to produce efficient leadership. Rather than 'a medicinable eye', to Thersites he becomes a 'botchy core', symbol of the diseases that infect the body politic (II.1.1). Not even good at marshalling the Greek troops, his call to action reads like a roll call of Greek casualties (V.5.11). It is with a huge sigh of relief that he hears of the death of Hector. He is right in thinking that Troy is doomed, but will disunity among the Greeks end?

## Ulysses

Often described as a wise elder statesman, Ulysses is constantly battling against individuals for whom the security of the state has lost its importance. His magnificent speech on Order is persuasive finely orchestrated rhetoric that seeks the support of generals and princes for 'specialty of rule'.

As often as not Ulysses fails to practice what he preaches—creating a credibility gap which may cost him his grip on the situation. His setting up of the fake lottery fosters emulation rather than degree. Ulysses, however, is pragmatic. The 'soul of the state' being secured, all else is relative—again, situation ethics. Although he dislikes Achilles intensely (I.3.369–70). Ulysses knows Ajax is his inferior, and is concerned not so much with 'plucking down Achilles's plumes' as with stinging him into action.

He combats Achilles's pride because he sincerely believes it breeds evil and division (I.3.317). Were Achilles not so difficult and awkward, there would have been no need to start an advertising compaign in Ajax's favour (I.3.381). As a manipulator of opinion, he thinks his

methods are valid in the circumstances. That his plans misfire is due
to his underestimating Polyxena's hold on Achilles.

He is usually a shrewd reader of character. His impressionistic
portraits of Troilus and Cressida, and his working on the rivalry of
Ajax and Achilles show this. To Troilus and Achilles he offers particularly bitter medicine. Does he derive pleasure in disillusioning them?
He manouevres Troilus out of his infatuation, and Achilles out of his
self-sufficiency. With Troilus he seems to be a kindly mentor and guide,
but he relishes the surprise Achilles gets when he informs him that his
'secret' dealings are the gossip of the camp and will soon reach the
islands:

> And all the Greekish girls shall tripping sing
> 'Great Hector's sister did Achilles win,
> But our great Ajax bravely beat down him'.
>
> (III.3.211)

Ulysses's cruel streak is shown when he repeats in detail Patroclus's
mimickry of the generals' failings and defects, and when he makes fun
of Ajax's pretensions. Ulysses is also a trickster having his own back
on those who slander 'mappery, closet war'. Though realising the
importance of brute force, his total admiration is for those who 'with
the fineness of their souls' control force by policy and stratagem.

It is this gift for policy that makes him manipulate the beef-witted
warlords. It is with obvious relish that he nourishes his plan:

> I have a young conception in my brain;
> Be you my time to bring it to some shape.
>
> (I.3.312)

Much to Thersites's satisfaction, his plans are 'proved not worth a
blackberry' (V.4.11), and it is his echo, Nestor, who prods Achilles into
action (V.5.17).

Ulysses himself has to admit that Achilles's brute force can change
defeat into victory: 'O courage, courage, princes! great Achilles / Is
arming.' (V.5.30) The irony of the situation lies in the fact that Hector
will be beaten by treachery and not by force. Achilles takes a leaf out
of Ulysses's war note-book. His treacherous instructions to the Myrmidons act out to the letter Ulysses's insistence on 'the still and mental
parts / That do contrive how many hands shall strike / When fitness
calls them on.' (I.3.200)

# War

## Achilles

Finally, Achilles comes to stand for treachery. Initially he stands for
the individuality that breeds division. He sulks in his tent, refusing to
acknowledge Agamemnon's authority, refusing to aid the Greek war
effort. He despises Greek policy, and undermines authority by inviting
Patroclus's satiric pageants of his superiors.

He has his own private reasons for keeping out of the war. Love has
unmanned him. His great affection for the effeminate Patroclus
(III.3.218), and his love for Polyxena have thrown him into a lethargy.
'Weak wanton Cupid' (III.3.222) has disarmed him, as Helen has Paris.
Despite this, Achilles thinks he can derive praise and respect for past
military glory. Ulysses describes him as 'plaguy proud':

> ... imagined worth
> Holds in his blood such swollen and hot discourse
> That 'twixt his mental and his active parts
> Kingdom'd Achilles in commotion rages
> And batters down himself.
>
> (II.3.170)

Ulysses's 'derision medicinable' (III.3.44) tries to educate Achilles to
the ravages of time on reputation. The 'selling' of Ajax as the new
Greek champion rankles within him (II.1.121). Achilles argued that
Hector 'knew his man' (II.1.127). He feels sure that his destiny is
linked to Hector's.

Proclaimed 'great' by friend and foe, his star on the ascendant while
that of Achilles declines, Hector naturally draws the envy of Achilles,
who wants to see his natural enemy at close range:

> I have a woman's longing,
> An appetite that I am sick withal,
> To see great Hector in his weeds of peace.
>
> (III.3.237)

This crisis of confidence sets him brooding and Hector's chivalry,
courtesy and greatness unsettle him:

> My mind is troubled like a fountain stirred,
> And I myself see not the bottom of it.
>
> (III.3.308)

After Hector's 'maiden battle' with Ajax, Achilles's longing becomes an obsession. Even Hector feels uncomfortable under his oppressing stare. Achilles's insolent outburst marks out Hector as his victim:

> Tell me, you heavens, in which part of his body
> Shall I destroy him?—whether there, or there, or there?
> (IV.5.242)

Having deftly snatched the initiative, Achilles emerges again into prominence. He is marked by a new strain of bloodthirstiness:

> I'll heat his blood with Greekish wine tonight,
> Which with my scimitar I'll cool tomorrow.
> Patroclus, let us feast him to the height.
> (V.1.1.)

The descent has started. It is perhaps significant that it is at this stage that Thersites accuses Patroclus of being Achilles's 'masculine whore and Achilles a hypocrite, 'a picture of what thou seemest' (V.1.3:17).

When stung by Patroclus's death, Achilles breaks his promise to Polyxena and goes into action. Out of practice and easily winded, he is spared his life by Hector's 'vice of mercy', which seems to insult his pride even further:

> I do disdain thy courtesy, proud Trojan.
> (V.6.15)

This shock clears his mind. Accepting his degradation, he finally contrives how many hands shall strike 'when fitness calls' them on:

> Come here about me, you my Myrmidons;
> Mark what I say. Attend me where I wheel;
> Strike not a stroke, but keep yourselves in breath,
> And when I have the bloody Hector found
> Empale him with your weapons round about.
> (V.7.1)

When he tracks down the unarmed Hector, he ruthlessly orders his Myrmidons 'Strike, fellows, strike; this is the man I seek.' Hector is murdered and Achilles's reputation among the Greeks safeguarded. Then with Ulysses's advice about opinion still ringing in his ears, he decides to start a publicity campaign. Compounding treachery with dishonesty, he markets this despicable gang-murder as fair combat:

> On Myrmidons, and cry you all amain,
> Achilles hath the mighty Hector slain.
> (V.8.13)

## Ajax

Ajax is initially presented as a selfwilled, envious bully whose main function is to 'plough up the wars'. Blockish, his vocabulary is restricted to repetitive name-calling—dog, cur, dog, cur, bitch wolf's son, cur—and empty threats. He is an obvious satiric target, and it is no wonder that even Thersites regards his choice as new Greek champion as 'patchery, juggling and knavery' (II.3.70).

Above all, Ajax does not know himself. However, as rival to Achilles, he is 'dressed up in voices', proclaimed wise and even 'adopted' as Nestor's son. When Thersites and Patroclus enact the 'pageant of Ajax' his character is further tarnished. He has become so proud, argues Thersites, that he is 'a very landfish, languageless, a monster' (III.3.262).

But when Ajax next appears on the stage, he is transformed. Alexander had earlier described him as a man of 'crowded humours', a strange mixture of virtues and vices, (I.2.23). It is the better side of his 'humours' that now emerges. His encounter with Hector brings out his courtesy and discretion:

> Thou art too gentle and too free a man.
> If I might in entreaties find success,
> As seld I have the chance, I would desire
> My famous cousin to our Grecian tents.
> (IV.5.139:149)

Is this the same Ajax? He has, ironically enough, acquired wisdom. He even acts as peace-maker, and buffer between Hector's wrath and Achilles's insolence (IV.5.261–6). After the gang-murder of Hector, it is he who first sees through Achilles's publicity campaign. In subdued notes he sounds the Greek-Trojan funeral lament:

> If it be so, yet bragless let it be;
> Great Hector was as good a man as he.
> (V.9.5)

## Hector

When the play starts, Hector is reported as a warrior in crisis. Vulnerable to the demands of honour, he has been 'fasting and waking' (I.2.35). His patience 'as a virtue fixed was moved today', because he had been struck down in battle by his cousin-german Ajax. Hector goes early to battle to retrieve his 'lost' honour:

> And to the field goes he; where every flower
> Did, as a prophet, weep what it foresaw
> In Hector's wrath.
>
> (I.2.9)

There is anticipation in Alexander's description. This search for honour will cost Hector his life. During a meeting of the Greek council, Aeneas comes trumpeting the chivalry of Hector who stands for the glory of Troy (I.3.235–7).

On stage, Hector is first seen debating an answer to the Greeks' carefully worded invitation to surrender Helen. There is no hint of disrespect, or 'base compulsion' in Nestor's formula. If there were, it would have been instantly rejected. As a responsible leader, therefore, Hector shows his humanity and clear-sightedness by arguing that Helen's value had been exaggerated, saying that, 'it is idolatry to make the service greater than the god' (II.2.56). He also argues it is a 'bad cause' (II.2.116), and that natural law is on the side of the Greeks. He debates not what is practical but what is moral in absolute terms:

> Thus to persist
> In doing wrong extenuates not wrong,
> But makes it much more heavy. Hector's opinion
> Is this in way of truth.
>
> (II.2.186)

Then comes the sudden turn-about and descent to expediency that have puzzled commentators:

> Yet, nevertheless,
> My sprightly brethren, I propend to you
> In resolution to keep Helen still;
> For 'tis a cause that hath no mean dependence
> Upon our joint and several dignities.
>
> (II.2.189)

Why does Hector do it? It is arguable that it would be equally wrong to surrender Helen against her will—she is obviously happy in Troy. Hector is not convinced by Troilus's arguments—he dismisses them as the 'hot passion of distempered blood' (II.2.169). It is Hector's spirit of loyalty to his side even in a 'bad cause' that forces his hand. As opposed to Troilus, Hector is more altruistic—he stresses 'joint and several dignities.' Knowing of Hector's later insistence on chivalry and honour, what is surprising is not this sudden change of mind, but his initial attempt to 'Let Helen go.'

Hector had already sent his challenge for single combat to the Greek camp. As suggested in Book VII of Homer's *Iliad*, a duel could have resolved the problem of honour without general bloodshed. In thus offering himself, Hector shows his humanity and generosity.

Partly because of guilt arising because 'the goodness of the quarrel' (II.2.123) is in doubt, Hector has developed his 'vice of mercy' and fair-play beyond limits which can prove dangerous. Nestor obviously admires his chivalry:

> That I have said to some my standers-by
> 'Lo, Jupiter is yonder, dealing life!'
>
> (IV.5.190)

Only rarely does Hector fall from courtesy. Realising his mistake in mentioning Menelaus's 'quondam wife' he is quick to apologise. His courtesy in the Greek camp is catching and the generals go out of their way to make themselves pleasant.

After the night of 'shapes of slaughter', hedged in by prophecy, he becomes the centre of action, his fall equated with that of Troy, as Cassandra forecasts (V.3.60). Hector senses danger but must honour his commitments:

> Life every man holds dear; but the dear man
> Holds honour far more precious-dear than life.
>
> (V.3.26)

Ironically, despite their promises, Achilles and Ajax have already decided against fighting. Hector feels he cannot 'break his faith' and goes to battle. As a warrior, he has no equal on the battlefield: 'There is a thousand Hectors in the field.' (V.5.19) But a combination of fair play, appetite, and rashness leads to his death. He spares Thersites, mistakenly spares Achilles, but then, infected by a dread strain from the sources, [both Dictys and Caxton describe how the Greek King Menon accused Hector of being 'a wolf ravysshyng and insacyable'] Hector contradicts in action his chivalric ideal and hunts the 'knight in sumptuous armour' for his 'hide' (V.6.30). Having contradicted the code of values by which he lives, Hector is brutally murdered and mutilated. Achilles, taking up Cassandra's prophecy, foretells the doom of Troy: 'So, Ilion, fall thou next! now, Troy, sink down.' (V.8.11)

## Cassandra

Cassandra appears twice in the play, at very decisive moments.

She first interrupts the Trojan council to foretell the doom of Troy in a very general way. Her symbolic utterance 'our firebrand brother burns us all' hardly has any effect on the outcome of the debate. When she next appears in V.3., her ability, visually and aurally, accurately to translate future events into the present is evident:

> Look how thou diest! Look how thy eye turns pale!
> Look how thy wounds do bleed at many vents! . . .
> Behold, distraction, frenzy, and amazement,
> Like witless antics, one another meet
> And all cry 'Hector! Hector's dead! O Hector!'
>
> (V.3.81)

Her function here, and in the earlier scene, is to assert unequivocally the fatalistic element that underlies much of the language and imagery of the play. Once she has made the direct statement, sounds and events prove her right. The chaotic distraction of the last three scenes acts out Cassandra's vision. Her phrase 'Hector's dead', 'Hector's slain' is repeated eight times in fifty lines.

# Deflation

## Thersites

Perhaps the most unwholesome character in Shakespeare, Thersites amused Achilles, who called him 'my cheese, my digestion'. Although he is called a 'privileged man', there is little of the traditional court jester in him. His humour is unpleasant, his vision is diseased, and he is a malcontent. Thersites's function is not to advance the plot, but to deflate Greek pretensions by a consistent distortion of motives. He slanders the Greeks and prevents the audience from feeling any sympathy for them. Imprecations, universal threats and curses come thick and fast from this immoral vivisector of motives:

> Vengeance on the whole camp! or, rather, the Neapolitan bone-ache! for that, methinks, is the curse dependent on those that war for a placket.
>
> (II.3.17)

His fitting the punishment to the crime, syphilis for promiscuity, and his persistent cursing of lechery might suggest he possesses some moral fervour (V.2.194–6). He also takes up Ulysses's image of 'appetite an universal wolf' (I.3.121) in his running commentary on the duel between Diomed and Troilus:

I think they have swallowed one another. I would laugh at that
miracle; yet in a sort lechery eats itself.

(V.4.31)

That is a profound thing to say. Yet Thersites, rather than being a
moral spokesman, is a malevolent atom, corrupt and corrupting. He
has no claim to be a moral healer. The poet Samuel Taylor Coleridge
(1772–1834) calls him a man of 'intellectual power deserted by all
grace.'

Not one Greek escapes his censure. Ajax and Achilles are oxen 'to
plough up the wars', Agamemnon is a 'botchy core', Nestor and Ulysses
'swearing rascals', Diomed 'a false-hearted rogue', Patroclus a 'masculine whore', Menelaus beyond contempt: 'I care not to be the louse
of a lazar, so I were not Menelaus.' (V.1.63)

His incessant scorn, counterpointing the long fine speeches of the
play, reduces the concepts of love, politics and war to their lowest
common denominator: 'All the argument is a cuckold and a whore.'
(II.3.71) Reduction of concepts is followed by a reduction of characters.
Early he associates characters with filthy beasts, but increasingly he
also uses reification, a method that consistently converts people to
things. Patroclus becomes a 'skein of sleave-silk, . . . a sarcenet flap . . .
a tassel' (V.1.30). These images emphasise Patroclus's effeminacy and
help to drive home the charge that he is Achilles's 'masculine whore'
(V.1.17). Cressida is described as a 'whetstone' that sharpens Diomed's
lust (V.2.76), Diomed becomes 'the sleeve' he's given (V.4.24), and
Menelaus the traditional symbol for cuckolds—horns (V.7.12).

That Thersites is twice spared his life is no indication that Shakespeare
had any sympathy for him—'thyself upon thyself', as Thersites would
say (II.3.26). His dismissal is ignominious. He not only admits to
physical cowardice, but his shameful surrender sounds like another
inverted litany: 'bastard begot, bastard instructed, bastard in mind,
bastard in valour, in everything illegitimate.' (V.7.17)

## Pandarus

Pandarus is another agent for deflation. Only Troilus and Ulysses are
allotted more lines than he. He merits inclusion in the second 1609
Quarto title-page: 'the conceited wooing of Pandarus, Prince of Licia.'

He furthers the action by bringing the lovers together but his power
in manipulating the love-plot is severely restricted by situation. His
traditional function is to 'sell' the lovers to each other. He also acts as
witness and priest in the mock ceremonies of bethrothal and marriage.

He insists Cressida must not be idealised, continually deflating Troilus's attempt to spiritualise her. Using 'vulgar' imagery of baking, he insists Cressida is a commodity to be consumed—like a 'cake of wheat'. (I.1.15)

There is a touch of blasphemy in Pandarus, and, traditionally, excessive contempt has been reserved for him. Yet in many ways he is a tender-hearted rogue, showing warmth and real sympathy for Troilus and Cressida (III.2.103) (IV.2.74–76). But Pandarus was not just the 'Prince of Licia'. As noun and verb, the word *pandar* had come to assume an independent existence. It implied a pimp, a bawd, a seller of flesh. Therefore after he pushes Troilus into Cressida's bed, Pandarus starts to assume this traditional role:

> And Cupid grant all tongue-tied maidens here
> Bed, chamber, pandar, to provide this gear!
>
> (III.2.209)

His snatches of lewd song stress his role of universal pandar, one song particularly, with its subtle word-play on 'die', acting out seduction on the stage (III.1.121–26). It is therefore not surprising that Thersites's curse—syphilis or the bone-ache for those who deal in prostitution—should escape the Greek camp and fall on Pandarus:

> such an ache in my bones that, unless a man were cursed, I cannot tell what to think on't.
>
> (V.3.101)

As carrier of disease, he deserves his shameful dismissal.

There are indications that his 'salacious epilogue' may not have formed part of Shakespeare's original intention. As it is, Pandarus holds the stage till the very end. This does not mean, however, as Harbage and Kimbrough have suggested,* that 'here and here only, in Shakespearian drama are the false and the treacherous riding high on Fortune's wheel at the end.' That may apply to Cressida and Achilles, but it does not apply to Pandarus. He has been dismissed. It is as the disillusioned broker, the dismissed pimp, that he has the last word. He is diseased, the boneache has got him. His tag of song ended, sweating and vainly 'seeking about for eases', he stands as an example for the rest. After his address he crawls away in shame.

---

* Alfred Harbage, *Shakespeare and the Rival Traditions*, Macmillan, New York, 1952, p.117.
Robert Kimbrough, *Shakespeare's Troilus and Cressida and its setting*, Harvard University Press, Cambridge, Mass., 1964, p.66.

# Style

Around 1601–3, Shakespeare was exploring ambiguous moral problems relating to conduct that admitted of different interpretations. However, in plays such as *All's Well*, *Hamlet*, and *Measure for Measure*, there is an appearance of solution and adjustment in the final act.

*Troilus and Cressida*, in contrast, insists on missing true poetic justice as far as the main culprits—Cressida and Achilles—are concerned. This is further complicated by Pandarus's unpleasant attack on the audience in the epilogue.

The several lines of the plot are neatly gathered, but the moral problems relating to love and war are not satisfactorily resolved. The ending, unique in Shakespeare, is inconclusive. There is no solution and no adjustment.

Shakespeare seems to be insisting that life can often be very untidy, and he deliberately sets out to deflate epic heroes and romantic ideals. This often required a juxtaposition of opposing attitudes, and quick changes of mood and method. Within general movements there are strong counter-currents. Comic and serious, romance and burlesque, tragic and satiric, high and low styles intermix and clash. This occurs throughout, and not just towards the end where the 'epilogue' has often predetermined critical interpretation.

However, it is not this agile shifting of the weights, the 'dexteritie' to which the 1609 Quarto epistle refers, that makes the temper of *Troilus and Cressida* so unique and so difficult to interpret. Moods grow out of and are made to clash with their opposite. For example, Troilus's idealistic vision of Cressida as 'stubborn chaste' in I.1 is immediately contrasted with Cressida's own realistic portrayal of the calculating bawdy coquette in I.2. The boorish Ajax is, after his mock 'adoption', immediately transformed into a model of behaviour. This often necessitates a shift of focus. The action is seen through the eyes of several characters, the point-of-view shifts continuously. This is in contrast to what happens in Shakespeare's other plays. In *Troilus and Cressida*, this occurs not only because of the several strands within the plot but also as a direct result of Shakespeare's attempt to observe character and action dispassionately. This is most evident in Cressida's betrayal scene (V.2), where several layers of comment and angles of vision help distance the action and make for dispassionate analysis.

Deflation, irony and satire inhabit the gap created between heroic claims and actual performance, between status and person, what a person seems and what he is. A character's claim to power or virtue is rapidly followed by a tearing-down, a puncturing of pretension. Thus both Helen and Cressida are described as 'pearl', but both are later castigated as whores. Achilles thinks he stands for valour but must resort to cowardly treachery. Ulysses preaches degree but manipulates envy and rivalry. Agamemnon basks in god-sun-king imagery and metaphor, but falls lamentably short of profession, symbol or status. Earlier expectations are not fulfilled, and these 'suspect centres' are, sooner or later, revealed.

The establishing, building-up and systematic debunking of these central figures is accomplished not only through action but also through language and imagery. Troilus's first appearance reveals not only his love of rhetoric but, through imagery, reveals also his romantic idealism, just as later (III.2) it will establish his sensuality. The verse too is cleverly modulated to fit his mood. Pandarus's vulgar bawdy comparison of making love to the several stages of making a wheat cake stresses his materiality. Character is linked to image. Cressida's bawdy imagery and word-play undercut Troilus's idealised metaphor of her. Thersites's scurrility and Pandarus's obscene tags of song contrast strongly with the serious philosophical debates and patterns of oratory in both Greek and Trojan councils. The comic prose is designed to lower the emotional tone of the early scenes, while the serious verse is meant to suit the mind of the 'wise' or 'earnest' figures.

The vicious satire of Thersites characterises the play. On the other hand, the Trojan debate on 'value' (Act II, Scene 2) and Ulysses's speech on Order and Degree (Act I, Scene 3 ll.75–137) can be read as models of traditional oratory, containing all the formal colours of rhetoric.

Language also establishes the fatalistic strain that runs throughout the play. Many characters speak as if they know it has already happened. The foresight of Calchas and Cassandra is catching. The doom of Troy is hinted at even by the non-dreamers Alexander, Cressida, Ulysses, Hector and finally even Troilus. Cressida's disloyalty is glimpsed in the curious negative similes that she uses 'as false as air . . . as fox to lamb', and in Pandarus's significant slip: 'Let all constant men be Troiluses, all false women Cressids.' (III.2.201)

Language is necessarily supported by symbol and imagery. Animal and disease imagery, for example, abound in Thersites's satire. Thersites not only associates man with the vilest animals but positively enjoys diagnosing the diseases that infect the body politic. His first appearance, and his recurrent use of vocabulary in the register of disease—boil, plague, red murrain, botchy core, itch, scab—establish his employment of making the Greeks more loathsome than they need be: 'I would thou didst itch from head to foot and I had the scratching of thee; I would make thee the loathsomest scab in Greece' (II.1.26)

Imagery is linked to movement—division, disintegration, and collapse. We are told that 'Kingdom'd Achilles rages and batters down himself'; at Cressida's betrayal 'the bonds of heaven are slipped, dissolved and loosed'; Ulysses's 'degree' speech abounds with verbs which anticipate the concrete chaotic scenes on the battlefield at the end of the play:

> Commotion in the winds, frights, changes, horrors,
> Divert and crack, rend and deracinate
> The unity and married calm of states.
>
> (I.3.98)

Indeed the language, imagery and movement anticipate Troilus's final disillusions. This occurs because, despite elements of parody and the mock-heroic framework, there is also a movement towards symbolic action. In the consistent inversion of the sacred there is also a hint of blasphemy that enforces this action.

For Thersites, curses are equivalent to prayers: 'I have said my prayers; and devil Envy say Amen' (II.3.20). Pandarus also uses the formulae and rituals of Christian tradition for betrothal and marriage, but these are undercut by manner and environment:

> Go to, a bargain made. Seal it, seal it. I'll be the witness. Here I hold your hand; here my cousin's . . . let all constant men be Troiluses, all false women Cressids, and all brokers-between Pandars! Say 'amen'.
>
> (III.2.196)

This counter-culture fits in with the mood of the play which also subverts traditional conceptions of chivalry, honour and love. Like Pandarus and Thersites, Shakespeare hits at the underside of love and war. But there is also an element of didacticism. The hunting of the knight 'in sumptuous armour' and the consequent murder of Hector read like a mediaeval *exemplum*: 'Most putrefied core, so fair without'—a miniature sermon in the midst of blasphemy or irreligion. Read in this way, Paris's earlier suggestion that Helen's 'white enchanting fingers' should help 'disarm great Hector' (III.1.155) stops being an irrelevant false start and becomes a signpost, directing readers and audiences towards the complexity and ambiguity on which the play thrives.

# Part 4

# Hints for study

FOR A BETTER understanding of *Troilus and Cressida*, key points and scenes demand close reading and more detailed study. An outline of units relating to theme, character and action provides a basis for valid argument.

## Theme

Seeming against Being. This reveals the hollowness of characters whose claim to power or virtue is not justified:

(1) **Agamemnon** is compared to the Sun whose 'medicinable eye' claims healing powers. Thersites, however, sees Agamemnon as a 'botchy core', a centre for disease. What is the effect of this criticism?

(2) **Helen** claims divinity as 'love's indivisible soul'. Hector argues she is 'not worth what she doth cost the holding'. Diomed describes her as 'contaminated carrion weight', and Thersites states the war is waged over 'a cuckold and a whore'. Why do Paris and Troilus argue that she is 'a theme of honour and renown'?

(3) **Cressida** is seen by Troilus as 'stubborn chaste' and invested with the 'eye of majesty'. Later she admits that 'the error of our eye directs our mind'. After he uncovers Cressida's lechery, Thersites points out that her 'mind is now turned whore'.

(4) **Achilles** is 'possessed with greatness'. He is proclaimed 'the sinew and the forehand' of the Greek army, but Ulysses claims that his 'imagined worth' has inflated his pride. After he is spared his life through Hector's 'vice of mercy', he engineers the brutal gang murder of Hector. Does he deserve the title of 'great-sized coward'?

(5) **Hector** hunts the knight in sumptuous armour as a 'goodly mark', but the victim turns out to be a 'putrefied core'. Why can this incident be read as the allegorical core of the play?

# Turning points

These often reveal character and determine the action:

(1) Hector argues that Helen must be surrendered 'in way of truth', but he 'nevertheless' maintains her continued defence for the Trojans' 'joint and several dignities'. Is his challenge to single combat an attempt to prevent general bloodshed?

(2) Cressida doubts whether she can be faithful to Troilus: 'I have a kind of self resides with you / But an unkind self, that itself will leave / To be another's fool.' When she gives in to Diomed, Troilus's love and worship change to rashness and revenge.

(3) Cassandra's prophecy is so strong that it determines the outcome of the final battle and death of Hector. During the last scenes her cry 'Hector, Hector's dead' is echoed and re-echoed by Greeks and Trojans.

(4) Achilles refuses to fight after reading Polyxena's message, but changes his mind after the slaying of Patroclus. He instructs his Myrmidons in treachery after being outraged by Hector's 'vice of mercy'.

# Close reading of parallel scenes

These aid the understanding of recurring themes:

(1) Act 1, Scene 3. and Act II, Scene 2. These are the Greek and Trojan debates for 'Order and Degree', against appetite and disorder. The 'imagined worth' of Achilles and Helen is discussed. Do these scenes constitute the philosophical centre of the play?

(2) Act III, Scene 2. and Act V, Scene 2. Contrast the love-scene of Troilus and Cressida, with the betrayal-scene of Diomed and Cressida. What is the effect of the watchers and eavesdroppers on the tone of both these scenes?

(3) Act I, Scene 2. Cressida's bawdy word-play deflates Troilus's romantic ideals. Act II, Scene 1. Thersites's scurrility deflates chivalry and heroic action.

(4) The Prologue and Pandarus's satiric epilogue effectively ring heroic action and tragic events within a deflationary framework. Why should this result in ambiguity?

(5) Compare Paris's suggestion to Helen to help 'disarm Hector' at the end of Act III, Scene 1. with Hector 'disarming' himself to better possess the 'sumptuous armour' in Act V, Scene 8. Do these constitute the temptations of Hector?

(6) Act V, Scene 2. and Act V, Scene 8. The climaxes of love-plot and war-plot respectively. What light do these scenes throw on the character of Troilus and Hector?

(7) Is Ulysses's admiration in Act I, Scene 3 for the 'still and mental parts' that determine 'how many hands shall strike' reflected in the treachery of Achilles? In Act V, Scene 7 Achilles instructs: 'Strike not a stroke but keep yourselves in breath'; in Act V, Scene 8 he orders: 'Strike fellows, strike, this is the man I seek.'

Even these three headings—Theme, Turning Points, and Parallel Scenes—carry a vast number of hints which can be used in examinations. Suitably adapted, they can form the basis for many essays.

# Answering questions

(1) Read the examination paper and instructions carefully.

(2) A three or four minute plan, sketching out the bare details, prevents needless repetition, and makes for clear presentation and a balanced logical argument. If you are asked, say, to examine the character of Troilus, it will be useful to list a number of points:

> Troilus's youth and his infatuation as a lover
> his use of sensual imagery
> his idealism
> his public and private image
> his defence of Helen in debate
> his fear for Cressida
> his proverbial constancy
> his disillusion and revenge
> his valour in battle
> his assumption of Trojan leadership

(3) Use short quotations to support your argument, and to link your argument to Shakespeare's text. Do not use long quotations unless you intend to analyse the language structure or imagery. Quotations should never be used as a substitute for argument.

(4) Answer all parts of the question. If you are asked to compare, say, the functions of Thersites and Pandarus, allow roughly equal weight to both characters, and throughout stress their function in the play.

(5) Write your answer in the form of an essay. Your introduction should examine the question in a general way. Each key point should then be dealt with in a separate paragraph. If possible, paragraphs should follow each other logically. A concluding paragraph should sum up your position.

(6) The following 'model' essays are based on the hints given above. A student is not expected to 'reproduce' them. They are intended to help the student to provide his own aids to better argument.

---

**Discuss the element of deflation in the characterisation and action of *Troilus and Cressida*.**

---

In Homer, Chaucer, and Lydgate the wrath of Achilles, the love of Troilus, and the death of Hector are romantic, tragic and heroic. In contrast, in Shakespeare's *Troilus and Cressida* these elements are considerably deflated.

Shakespeare invests characters with 'inherited' virtue or power. Gradually he punctures their pretence to greatness, revealing a gap between what they claim to be and what they are. Thus Troilus attributes to Cressida 'the eye of majesty'; Agamemnon is compared to the Sun whose 'medicinable eye' heals evil; Helen's beauty, we learn, 'hath launched above a thousand ships'. An eye or a face is enough to start a crusade.

This build-up sustains the super-persons who feed on general respect and adulation, products of a tradition that insists on making 'the service greater than the god'. A re-assessment leads to deflation, irony and satire that expose the fragility of pretension.

In *Troilus and Cressida* the point-of-view shifts continuously. Thus, in her first scene, Cressida makes fun of Pandarus's selling of Troilus as 'prince of chivalry' but more effectively punctures her own image as idealised by Troilus in the previous scene. Instead of the virtuous 'stubborn chaste'. Cressida's indecent word-play reveals her as bawdy and lascivious. Agamemnon's pretensions to authority are also debunked. Aeneas sees him as a 'god in office guiding men', but he is inefficient and himself requires guidance. Shakespeare pokes fun at him. Counting on tradition, Aeneas had expected a dazzling 'youthful Phoebus' or Sun, but a dull and insignificant Agamemnon has to assure him:

> That thou shalt know, Trojan, he is awake
> He tells thee so himself.

This is what happens with Helen. When she appears once towards the middle of the play it is enough to destroy a tradition that had lasted for generations. The symbol, re-examined, is found peculiarly hollow — certainly not 'love's indivisible soul'.

All these characters, and others like Achilles who are possessed with 'imagined worth', maintain the satiric undercurrents that prevent a reading of *Troilus and Cressida* as straight tragedy on the traditionally epic theme of Troy. But the most consistent deflators, Thersites and Pandarus, are not conceived as admirable.

The envious Thersites is a 'privileged man' whose humour is always unpleasant. His muck-raking and satiric 'pageants' would have pleased the play-goers as they pleased Achilles. Thersites acts like a vile chorus, commenting bitterly on what is happening, unmasking trickery and deceit. His virulent speeches provide an effective counter-blast to the philosophical and moral disquisitions on 'degree', value and honour of Ulysses, Hector and Troilus. Thersites examines the soft underbelly of war, and his conclusion damns both sides. The quarrel is about 'a cuckold and a whore'.

Although he shows some sympathy towards the Trojans, not one Greek escapes his blistering censure. Thersites is best seen as an anti-Greek chorus. To him, Diomed is a 'dissembling abominable varlet' who sleeps with a 'dissembling luxurious drab'; Menelaus, for whose wounded honour the war is waged, is beyond contempt; for all his slyness, Ulysses's stratagems are proved 'not worth a blackberry'. Thersites inverts Ulysses's image of Agamemnon as 'medicinable eye' to make him a source of disease — 'a botchy core' infecting the army. Just as 'lechery' is his favourite word, 'disease' is his favourite register.

Through Thersites we see the limits of Cressida's falsity. In the seduction scene, he vividly translates Cressida's excuses — her 'mind is now turned whore', she becomes a 'whetstone' sharpening Diomed's lust.

Thersites has no pretensions to being a moral healer; Nestor describes him as a muck-raker whose 'gall coins slander like the mint', but Thersites's attacks are nearly always a reaction, violent and obscene, to an unpleasant reality. Although his unwarranted slur on the amiable Patroclus as Achilles's 'masculine whore' may sound like slander to discredit a beautiful friendship, Patroclus is presented as slightly effeminate.

The other deflator is Pandarus. Only Troilus and Ulysses are allotted more lines than he. He accelerates the action by bringing the lovers together, and acts as counter-balance to Troilus who is a typical romantic lover. To Troilus, Cressida is the 'cygnet's down', an Indian pearl. To Pandarus she is a wheaten cake, that must be consumed — after the necessary grinding, bolting, leavening and baking: 'nay you must stay the cooling too, or you may chance to burn your lips'.

Most significant is Pandarus's deflation of Helen. When in I.2. he recounts the incident of the 'white hair' on Troilus's chin, we know that 'Helen is a merry Greek indeed.' But it is in III.1. that he really helps to deflate this most central symbol of love and beauty. His words and crooning reduce Ilium to the level of a high-class brothel. His insistence in the song on the sexual meaning of 'die' that turns groans to laughter and excitement acts out Paris's and Helen's continued dissipation.

Coming as it does immediately prior to the love-night, this deflation throws a shadow of lust on the meeting of Troilus and Cressida. This is further complicated by Pandarus's subverting traditional formulas and Christian ritual for betrothal and marriage. 'I'll be the witness. Here I hold your hand; here my cousin's. Say Amen ... Amen'. He further lowers the tone of the love-scene by offering to provide a pandar for willing 'tongue-tied maidens' in the playhouse. His deflation in 'how go maidenheads?' is resented even by Cressida.

After the Antenor-Cressida exchange, Pandarus does little except curse the lovers' luck and worry about his failing health. When he annoys Troilus by appearing on the battlefield his dismissal is therefore as shameful as that of Thersites:

> Hence, broker-lackey! ignomy and shame
> Pursue they life, and live aye with thy name.

Although dismissed he has the last word on the stage. He is diseased and must 'seek about for eases'. He switches to song in an attempt to shrug off his dismissal, and then suddenly launches his own attack on part of the audience, 'brethren and sisters of the hold-door trade'.

There is some textual evidence that Pandarus had been originally dismissed in V.3. when he delivered Cressida's letter. As the play now stands, however, the dismissal and the 'epilogue' provide a strong satiric exit. Together with the Prologue, they bring the potentially tragic story — the disillusion of Troilus, and the death of Hector — within a mock-heroic framework.

---

**Discuss love and its influence on the war effort in *Troilus and Cressida*.**

---

There are two main strands in the plot of *Troilus and Cressida*: the love of Troilus, and the prodding of Achilles into battle which results in the tragic death of Hector. War is waged not because of territorial or trade disputes but because 'the ravished Helen, Menelaus's queen/With wanton Paris sleeps'.

There is dissension and corruption in both Greek camp and Trojan court. Both sides are war-weary. Ideals of chivalry and honour have lost their splendour through years of bickering. The 'privileged' Thersites satirises the origin and continuance of the war — the argument is 'a cuckold and a whore'. This is the most damaging appraisal, but even

Diomed dismissively argues that wealth, friends and years have been needlessly spent on a 'dishonoured' whore.

Motives for love and war undergo scrutiny. If the war has reached an impasse, love has been devalued to lust. Thersites invokes disease, especially the 'bone-ache' which is 'the curse dependent upon those that war for a placket'. Paris and Troilus, however, continue to support Helen as 'a theme of honour and renown', but Hector argues she is 'not worth what she doth cost the holding'. Although he later continues to defend their 'joint and several dignities', Hector realises Helen's danger to the Trojan war effort. She has lulled Paris into inaction. While soldiers and princes suffer, Paris has 'the honey still'. Paris, says Priam, speaks 'like one besotted'. This implies that Helen has impaired his capacity for reasoning.

In the only scene where she appears, Helen is presented in an unfavourable light. Her servant claims she is the 'heart-blood of beauty, love's indivisible soul', but she turns out to be a very silly woman indeed. Hector was right — the Trojans had given themselves to 'mad idolatry'. Throughout, the service has been 'greater than the god'. Although invested with divinity, she is an agent of lethargy. Even Paris admits this: 'I would fain have armed today but my Nell would not have it so'. As an embodiment of the traditional sublime, 'my Nell' runs close to the ridiculous.

Pandarus's song, acting out the love-chase and the seduction that follows, encapsulates Paris's and Helen's fascination with a love game that will destroy Troy: 'Let thy song be love; this love will undo us all'. In a different context, Cassandra had prophesied 'our firebrand brother burns us all'. Love then constitutes a danger. This is further stressed when Paris urges Helen to charm Hector more firmly on their side:

> ... His stubborn buckles,
> With those your white enchanting fingers touched,
> Shall more obey than to the edge of steel.

In some strange way, this temptation through beauty anticipates Hector's temptation to hunt the knight for his 'sumptuous armour'. But Hector remains a valiant warrior to the end.

Like Paris, Achilles keeps away from the battlefield. Ulysses 'educates' him to see that his infatuation for Polyxena, the daughter of the enemy, not only harms the 'soul of the state', but has damaged his reputation. Achilles's manliness is also weakened by his association with Patroclus, who is 'effeminate'. Thersites's remarks about his being Achilles's 'masculine whore' is intended to slander a beautiful friendship. But watching Patroclus's pageants 'on his pressed bed lolling' has not made Achilles a better or fitter warrior. Patroclus urges Achilles:

> Sweet, rouse yourself, and the weak wanton Cupid
> Shall from your neck unloose his amorous fold.

Seeing that his reputation is in danger, Achilles decides to re-enter the war. However, a letter and token from Polyxena make him shirk his duty: 'My major vow lies here; this I'll obey'. Only when his Myrmidons are slaughtered, and his beloved Patroclus slain, does Achilles shake off 'wanton Cupid' to seek out Hector in battle. But wantonness has weakened him. He is easly winded and only Hector's 'vice of mercy' spares his life. Unable to beat Hector fairly, he resorts to trickery and manoeuvres the gang-murder of Hector.

Troilus's love for Cressida is also initially a danger to his manhood. He describes himself repeatedly in female terms: 'weaker than a woman's tear', 'less valiant than the virgin in the night'. His frustrated love distracts his mind from the Trojan war effort. Despite Pandarus's deflation, Troilus idealises Cressida: 'Her bed is India, there she lies a pearl'. The temptation to escape from the war, to 'wallow in the lily fields', is there, but Troilus is deeply conscious of his public duties. Although divided, he does not allow love to rule his action, as Paris and Achilles do. Realising 'womanish it is to be from thence', he accompanies Aeneas to battle and fully deserves the people's acclaim.

Troilus's ideals of love and honour spur him to speak for continuing the war. He is absent from the Trojan council when the 'Antenor exchange' is debated. Having spent the night with Cressida, he does not question council's decision, and the demands of war take precedence over his personal relationship. At first he seems stunned, even takes up the role of 'priest' reconciled to his fate. But his love forces him away from withdrawal and inaction. To meet his Cressida every night, he will 'grow friend with danger'.

However, when the flighty Cressida crosses over to the Greeks, Troilus experiences the agony of treachery and is viciously jolted out of his previous idolatry. His goddess proved false, he now dedicates himself to ruthless slaughter.

In each case, love had led to ruin. In each case, will and passion had taken over from reason, unable to distinguish between right and wrong, and therefore leading to disorder. The wise Hector had spoken against 'raging appetite', and Ulysses's degree speech showed the disasters caused by uncontrolled desire. There is disorder in the heavens and chaos in society. Troilus himself believes that all is thrown into chaos when Cressida's 'o'er-eaten faith' is given to Diomed: 'The bonds of heaven are slipped, dissolved and loosed'.

That being so, he throws caution to the winds. Fighting for the 'sleeve', emblem of his betrayed love, he does 'mad and fantastic execution'. The murder of Hector increases his resentment. He knows Troy is doomed, and although Aeneas warns him that his words 'discomfort all the host', Troilus's love has been so twisted into hate that he can only promise the ravages of war:

> Strike a free march to Troy! with comfort go:
> Hope of revenge shall hide our inward woe.

# Part 5

# Suggestions for further reading

## The Text

WALKER, ALICE, ED.: *Troilus and Cressida* (The New Cambridge Shakespeare) Cambridge University Press, Cambridge, 1957. The best annotated edition. Quotations in these *Notes* refer to this edition.

## Useful Critical Studies

ASP, CAROLYN: 'Th'Expense of Spirit in a Waste of Shame', *Shakespeare Quarterly*, 22, 1971, 345–357.

BAYLEY, JOHN: 'Time and the Trojans', *Essays in Criticism*, 25, Oxford, 1975, 55–73.

BONJOUR, ADRIEN: 'Hector and the one in sumptuous armour', *English Studies*, 45, 1964, 104–108.

BULLOUGH, GEOFFREY: *Narrative and Dramatic Sources of Shakespeare*, Vol.VI, Routledge & Kegan Paul, London, 1966. Comprehensive discussion of most relevant sources for *Troilus and Cressida*. Much relevant material from Chapman's *Iliad*, Lydgate's *Troy-Book*, and Caxton's *Recuyell*.

CAMPBELL, O.J.: *Comicall Satyre and Shakespeare's Troilus and Cressida*, Huntingdon Library Publications, San Marino, 1938.

COGHILL, NEVILL: *Shakespeare's Professional Skills*, Cambridge University Press, Cambridge, 1964.

COX, JOHN D.: 'The Error of Our Eye in *Troilus and Cressida*', *Comparative Drama*, 10, 1976, 147–171.

DONALDSON, IAN: 'Double-Meanings — Shakespeare's Serious Indecency', *Essays in Criticism*, 24, 1974, 363–367.

FLY, R.D.: 'Cassandra and the Language of Prophecy', *Shakespeare Quarterly*, 26, 1975, 157–171.

KAULA, DAVID: 'Will and Reason in Troilus and Cressida', *Shakespeare Quarterly*, 12, 1961, 271–283.

KIMBROUGH, ROBERT: *Shakespeare's Troilus and Cressida and its Setting*, Harvard University Press, Cambridge, Mass., 1964. Contains an extensive bibliography.

KNIGHTS, L.C.: *'Troilus and Cressida* Again', *Scrutiny*, 18, 1951, 144–157.

LAWRENCE, W.W.: *Shakespeare's Problem Comedies*, Macmillan, New York, 1931.

NOSWORTHY, J.M.: *Shakespeare's Occasional Plays*, Edward Arnold, London, 1965.

NOWOTTNY, W.M.T.: 'Opinion and Value in *Troilus and Cressida*', *Essays in Criticism*, 4, 1954, 282–296.

OATES, J.C.: 'The Ambiguity of *Troilus and Cressida*', *Shakespeare Quarterly*, 17, 1966, 141–150.

RAMSEY, J.W.: 'The Provenance of *Troilus and Cressida*', *Shakespeare Quarterly*, 21, 1970, 223–240.

ROSSITER, A.P.: *Angel with Horns*, Longman, London, 1961.

SELTZER, DANIEL: *The History of Troilus and Cressida*, (Signet Classic Shakespeare) New York, 1963. Contains a sound introduction.

SOELLNER, R.: 'Prudence and the Price of Helen', *Shakespeare Quarterly*, 20, 1969, 255–263.

TILLYARD, E.W.M.: *Shakespeare's Problem Plays*, Chatto & Windus, London, 1950.

WHITAKER, VIRGIL: *Shakespeare's Use of Learning*, Huntingdon Library Publications, San Marino, 1964.

# The author of these notes

Dr DANIEL MASSA, who is a Senior Lecturer in English, Old University, Malta, was educated at the Universities of Exeter, Malta and Edinburgh. He is general editor of the *Journal of Mediterranean Studies*, 1978; he is also co-founder of the Xsenuru Experimental Drama Group. His poetry has been published in shared collections, among them *Kwartett*, 1966; *Analizi '70*, 1970; *Malta — The New Poetry*, 1971; *Linji Godda*, 1973; and *Limestone 84*, 1978. He has published critical articles in various journals, and was Organising Secretary of the Association for Commonwealth Literature and Language Studies 1978 conference. He has just edited *Individual and Community in Commonwealth Literature*, 1979.

# York Notes: list of titles

**CHINUA ACHEBE**
*A Man of the People*
*Arrow of God*
*Things Fall Apart*

**EDWARD ALBEE**
*Who's Afraid of Virginia Woolf?*

**ELECHI AMADI**
*The Concubine*

**ANONYMOUS**
*Beowulf*
*Everyman*

**AYI KWEI ARMAH**
*The Beautyful Ones Are Not Yet Born*

**W. H. AUDEN**
*Selected Poems*

**JANE AUSTEN**
*Emma*
*Mansfield Park*
*Northanger Abbey*
*Persuasion*
*Pride and Prejudice*
*Sense and Sensibility*

**HONORÉ DE BALZAC**
*Le Père Goriot*

**SAMUEL BECKETT**
*Waiting for Godot*

**SAUL BELLOW**
*Henderson, The Rain King*

**ARNOLD BENNETT**
*Anna of the Five Towns*
*The Card*

**WILLIAM BLAKE**
*Songs of Innocence, Songs of Experience*

**ROBERT BOLT**
*A Man For All Seasons*

**HAROLD BRIGHOUSE**
*Hobson's Choice*

**ANNE BRONTË**
*The Tenant of Wildfell Hall*

**CHARLOTTE BRONTË**
*Jane Eyre*

**EMILY BRONTË**
*Wuthering Heights*

**ROBERT BROWNING**
*Men and Women*

**JOHN BUCHAN**
*The Thirty-Nine Steps*

**JOHN BUNYAN**
*The Pilgrim's Progress*

**BYRON**
*Selected Poems*

**GEOFFREY CHAUCER**
*Prologue to the Canterbury Tales*
*The Clerk's Tale*
*The Franklin's Tale*
*The Knight's Tale*
*The Merchant's Tale*
*The Miller's Tale*
*The Nun's Priest's Tale*
*The Pardoner's Tale*
*The Wife of Bath's Tale*
*Troilus and Criseyde*

**SAMUEL TAYLOR COLERIDGE**
*Selected Poems*

**SIR ARTHUR CONAN DOYLE**
*The Hound of the Baskervilles*

**WILLIAM CONGREVE**
*The Way of the World*

**JOSEPH CONRAD**
*Heart of Darkness*
*Nostromo*
*Victory*

**STEPHEN CRANE**
*The Red Badge of Courage*

**BRUCE DAWE**
*Selected Poems*

**WALTER DE LA MARE**
*Selected Poems*

**DANIEL DEFOE**
*A Journal of the Plague Year*
*Moll Flanders*
*Robinson Crusoe*

**CHARLES DICKENS**
*A Tale of Two Cities*
*Bleak House*
*David Copperfield*
*Dombey and Son*
*Great Expectations*
*Hard Times*
*Little Dorrit*
*Oliver Twist*
*The Pickwick Papers*

**EMILY DICKINSON**
*Selected Poems*

**JOHN DONNE**
*Selected Poems*

**JOHN DRYDEN**
*Selected Poems*

**GERALD DURRELL**
*My Family and Other Animals*

**GEORGE ELIOT**
*Middlemarch*
*Silas Marner*
*The Mill on the Floss*

**T. S. ELIOT**
*Four Quartets*
*Murder in the Cathedral*
*Selected Poems*
*The Cocktail Party*
*The Waste Land*

**J. G. FARRELL**
*The Siege of Krishnapur*

**WILLIAM FAULKNER**
*Absalom, Absalom!*
*The Sound and the Fury*

**HENRY FIELDING**
*Joseph Andrews*
*Tom Jones*

**F. SCOTT FITZGERALD**
*Tender is the Night*
*The Great Gatsby*

**GUSTAVE FLAUBERT**
*Madame Bovary*

**E. M. FORSTER**
*A Passage to India*
*Howards End*

**JOHN FOWLES**
*The French Lieutenant's Woman*

**ATHOL FUGARD**
*Selected Plays*

**JOHN GALSWORTHY**
*Strife*

MRS GASKELL
  *North and South*
WILLIAM GOLDING
  *Lord of the Flies*
  *The Spire*
OLIVER GOLDSMITH
  *She Stoops to Conquer*
  *The Vicar of Wakefield*
ROBERT GRAVES
  *Goodbye to All That*
GRAHAM GREENE
  *Brighton Rock*
  *The Heart of the Matter*
  *The Power and the Glory*
WILLIS HALL
  *The Long and the Short and the Tall*
THOMAS HARDY
  *Far from the Madding Crowd*
  *Jude the Obscure*
  *Selected Poems*
  *Tess of the D'Urbervilles*
  *The Mayor of Casterbridge*
  *The Return of the Native*
  *The Trumpet Major*
  *The Woodlanders*
  *Under the Greenwood Tree*
L. P. HARTLEY
  *The Go-Between*
  *The Shrimp and the Anemone*
NATHANIEL HAWTHORNE
  *The Scarlet Letter*
SEAMUS HEANEY
  *Selected Poems*
JOSEPH HELLER
  *Catch-22*
ERNEST HEMINGWAY
  *A Farewell to Arms*
  *For Whom the Bell Tolls*
  *The Old Man and the Sea*
HERMANN HESSE
  *Steppenwolf*
BARRY HINES
  *Kes*
HOMER
  *The Iliad*
  *The Odyssey*
ANTHONY HOPE
  *The Prisoner of Zenda*
GERARD MANLEY HOPKINS
  *Selected Poems*
RICHARD HUGHES
  *A High Wind in Jamaica*
TED HUGHES
  *Selected Poems*
THOMAS HUGHES
  *Tom Brown's Schooldays*
ALDOUS HUXLEY
  *Brave New World*
HENRIK IBSEN
  *A Doll's House*
  *Ghosts*
HENRY JAMES
  *The Ambassadors*
  *The Portrait of a Lady*
  *Washington Square*
SAMUEL JOHNSON
  *Rasselas*
BEN JONSON
  *The Alchemist*
  *Volpone*
JAMES JOYCE
  *A Portrait of the Artist as a Young Man*
  *Dubliners*

JOHN KEATS
  *Selected Poems*
PHILIP LARKIN
  *Selected Poems*
D. H. LAWRENCE
  *Selected Short Stories*
  *Sons and Lovers*
  *The Rainbow*
  *Women in Love*
CAMARA LAYE
  *L'Enfant Noir*
HARPER LEE
  *To Kill a Mocking-Bird*
LAURIE LEE
  *Cider with Rosie*
THOMAS MANN
  *Tonio Kröger*
CHRISTOPHER MARLOWE
  *Doctor Faustus*
ANDREW MARVELL
  *Selected Poems*
W. SOMERSET MAUGHAM
  *Selected Short Stories*
GAVIN MAXWELL
  *Ring of Bright Water*
J. MEADE FALKNER
  *Moonfleet*
HERMAN MELVILLE
  *Moby Dick*
THOMAS MIDDLETON
  *Women Beware Women*
THOMAS MIDDLETON *and* WILLIAM ROWLEY
  *The Changeling*
ARTHUR MILLER
  *A View from the Bridge*
  *Death of a Salesman*
  *The Crucible*
JOHN MILTON
  *Paradise Lost I & II*
  *Paradise Lost IV & IX*
  *Selected Poems*
V. S. NAIPAUL
  *A House for Mr Biswas*
ROBERT O'BRIEN
  *Z for Zachariah*
SEAN O'CASEY
  *Juno and the Paycock*
GABRIEL OKARA
  *The Voice*
EUGENE O'NEILL
  *Mourning Becomes Electra*
GEORGE ORWELL
  *Animal Farm*
  *Nineteen Eighty-four*
JOHN OSBORNE
  *Look Back in Anger*
WILFRED OWEN
  *Selected Poems*
ALAN PATON
  *Cry, The Beloved Country*
THOMAS LOVE PEACOCK
  *Nightmare Abbey* and *Crotchet Castle*
HAROLD PINTER
  *The Caretaker*
SYLVIA PLATH
  *Selected Works*
PLATO
  *The Republic*
ALEXANDER POPE
  *Selected Poems*

J. B. PRIESTLEY
  *An Inspector Calls*
THOMAS PYNCHON
  *The Crying of Lot 49*
SIR WALTER SCOTT
  *Ivanhoe*
  *Quentin Durward*
  *The Heart of Midlothian*
  *Waverley*
PETER SHAFFER
  *The Royal Hunt of the Sun*
WILLIAM SHAKESPEARE
  *A Midsummer Night's Dream*
  *Antony and Cleopatra*
  *As You Like It*
  *Coriolanus*
  *Cymbeline*
  *Hamlet*
  *Henry IV Part I*
  *Henry IV Part II*
  *Henry V*
  *Julius Caesar*
  *King Lear*
  *Love's Labour's Lost*
  *Macbeth*
  *Measure for Measure*
  *Much Ado About Nothing*
  *Othello*
  *Richard II*
  *Richard III*
  *Romeo and Juliet*
  *Sonnets*
  *The Merchant of Venice*
  *The Taming of the Shrew*
  *The Tempest*
  *The Winter's Tale*
  *Troilus and Cressida*
  *Twelfth Night*
GEORGE BERNARD SHAW
  *Androcles and the Lion*
  *Arms and the Man*
  *Caesar and Cleopatra*
  *Candida*
  *Major Barbara*
  *Pygmalion*
  *Saint Joan*
  *The Devil's Disciple*
MARY SHELLEY
  *Frankenstein*
PERCY BYSSHE SHELLEY
  *Selected Poems*
RICHARD BRINSLEY SHERIDAN
  *The School for Scandal*
  *The Rivals*
R. C. SHERRIFF
  *Journey's End*
WOLE SOYINKA
  *The Road*
EDMUND SPENSER
  *The Faerie Queene* (Book I)
JOHN STEINBECK
  *Of Mice and Men*
  *The Grapes of Wrath*
  *The Pearl*

LAURENCE STERNE
  *A Sentimental Journey*
  *Tristram Shandy*
ROBERT LOUIS STEVENSON
  *Kidnapped*
  *Treasure Island*
TOM STOPPARD
  *Professional Foul*
  *Rosencrantz and Guildenstern are Dead*
JONATHAN SWIFT
  *Gulliver's Travels*
JOHN MILLINGTON SYNGE
  *The Playboy of the Western World*
TENNYSON
  *Selected Poems*
W. M. THACKERAY
  *Vanity Fair*
DYLAN THOMAS
  *Under Milk Wood*
FLORA THOMPSON
  *Lark Rise to Candleford*
J. R. R. TOLKIEN
  *The Hobbit*
ANTHONY TROLLOPE
  *Barchester Towers*
MARK TWAIN
  *Huckleberry Finn*
  *Tom Sawyer*
JOHN VANBRUGH
  *The Relapse*
VIRGIL
  *The Aeneid*
VOLTAIRE
  *Candide*
KEITH WATERHOUSE
  *Billy Liar*
EVELYN WAUGH
  *Decline and Fall*
JOHN WEBSTER
  *The Duchess of Malfi*
H. G. WELLS
  *The History of Mr Polly*
  *The Invisible Man*
  *The War of the Worlds*
OSCAR WILDE
  *The Importance of Being Earnest*
THORNTON WILDER
  *Our Town*
TENNESSEE WILLIAMS
  *The Glass Menagerie*
VIRGINIA WOOLF
  *Mrs Dalloway*
  *To the Lighthouse*
WILLIAM WORDSWORTH
  *Selected Poems*
WILLIAM WYCHERLEY
  *The Country Wife*
W. B. YEATS
  *Selected Poems*

# York Handbooks: list of titles

YORK HANDBOOKS form a companion series to York Notes and are designed to meet the wider needs of students of English and related fields. Each volume is a compact study of a given subject area, written by an authority with experience in communicating the essential ideas to students at all levels.

**AN INTRODUCTORY GUIDE TO ENGLISH LITERATURE**
*by* MARTIN STEPHEN
**PREPARING FOR EXAMINATIONS IN ENGLISH LITERATURE**
*by* NEIL McEWAN
**EFFECTIVE STUDYING**
*by* STEVE ROBERTSON *and* DAVID SMITH
**STYLE IN ENGLISH PROSE**
*by* NEIL McEWAN
**READING THE SCREEN**
*An Introduction to Film Studies*
*by* JOHN IZOD
**THE ENGLISH NOVEL**
*by* IAN MILLIGAN
**ENGLISH POETRY**
*by* CLIVE T. PROBYN
**DRAMA: PLAYS, THEATRE AND PERFORMANCE**
*by* MARGERY MORGAN
**ENGLISH USAGE**
*by* COLIN G. HEY
**ENGLISH GRAMMAR**
*by* LORETO TODD
**AN INTRODUCTION TO LINGUISTICS**
*by* LORETO TODD
**AN INTRODUCTION TO LITERARY CRITICISM**
*by* RICHARD DUTTON
**A DICTIONARY OF LITERARY TERMS**
*by* MARTIN GRAY
**STUDYING CHAUCER**
*by* ELISABETH BREWER
**STUDYING SHAKESPEARE**
*by* MARTIN STEPHEN *and* PHILIP FRANKS
**STUDYING MILTON**
*by* GEOFFREY M. RIDDEN
**STUDYING JANE AUSTEN**
*by* IAN MILLIGAN
**STUDYING THE BRÖNTES**
*by* SHEILA SULLIVAN
**STUDYING CHARLES DICKENS**
*by* K. J. FIELDING
**STUDYING THOMAS HARDY**
*by* LANCE ST JOHN BUTLER
**STUDYING JAMES JOYCE**
*by* HARRY BLAMIRES
**A CHRONOLOGY OF ENGLISH LITERATURE**
*by* MARTIN GRAY
**A DICTIONARY OF BRITISH AND IRİSH AUTHORS**
*by* ANTONY KAMM
**AN A.B.C. OF SHAKESPEARE**
*by* P. C. BAYLEY
**THE METAPHYSICAL POETS**
*by* TREVOR JAMES
**THE AGE OF ROMANTIC LITERATURE**
*by* HARRY BLAMIRES
**THE VICTORIAN AGE OF LITERATURE**
*by* HARRY BLAMIRES
**ENGLISH LITERATURE FROM THE THIRD WORLD**
*by* TREVOR JAMES